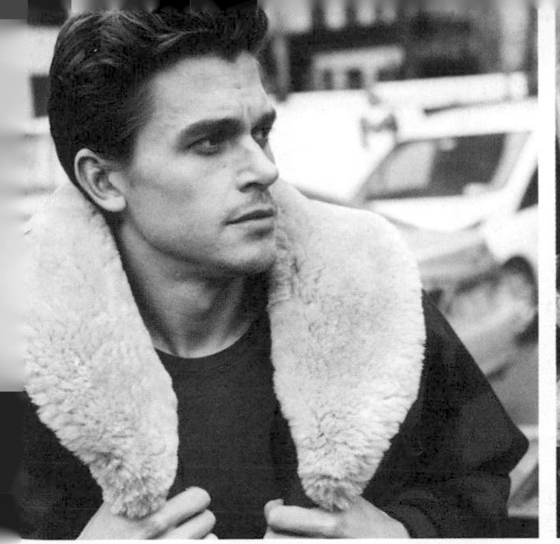

劉氏
218 WIN SEA FOOD MARKE

ANTONI
IN THE
KITCHEN

YOUR
EGO
FIRE ALARM
RATANIC
ARMY
NYC
KUSH
CO.
AKHENATEN
STREET
APHRODITE
Grafstract by
F.D.C.
SPRINKLER
THROUGHOUT
BUILDING

ANTONI IN THE KITCHEN

Antoni Porowski

WITH MINDY FOX

PHOTOGRAPHS BY PAUL BRISSMAN

A RUX MARTIN BOOK • HOUGHTON MIFFLIN HARCOURT • BOSTON NEW YORK 2019

Special thanks to the following locations in New York City:
Bedford Cheese Shop · *Associated Cut Flower Co., Inc.*
Fish Tales Gourmet Seafood Market · *Kiszka Meat Market*
La Colombe Coffee Roasters · *Village Den*

hmhbooks.com

Book design and hand lettering by Laura Palese

Food styling by Lisa Homa

Prop styling by Kristine Trevino

Library of Congress Cataloging-in-Publication Data

Names: Porowski, Antoni, author. | Fox, Mindy, author. | Brissman, Paul, photographer.

Title: Antoni in the kitchen / Antoni Porowski with Mindy Fox ; photographs by Paul Brissman.

Description: Boston : Houghton Mifflin Harcourt, [2019] | Includes index. | "A Rux Martin Book."

Identifiers: LCCN 2019002545 (print) | LCCN 2019002714 (ebook) | ISBN 9781328631350 (ebook) | ISBN 9781328631343 (paper over board) | 9780358206170 (special edition) | 9780358206187 (special edition)

Subjects: LCSH: Cooking. | LCGFT: Cookbooks.

Classification: LCC TX714 (ebook) | LCC TX714 .P6813 2019 (print) | DDC 641.5—dc23

LC record available at https://lccn.loc.gov/2019002545

Printed in China

SCP 10 9 8 7 6 5 4 3 2 1

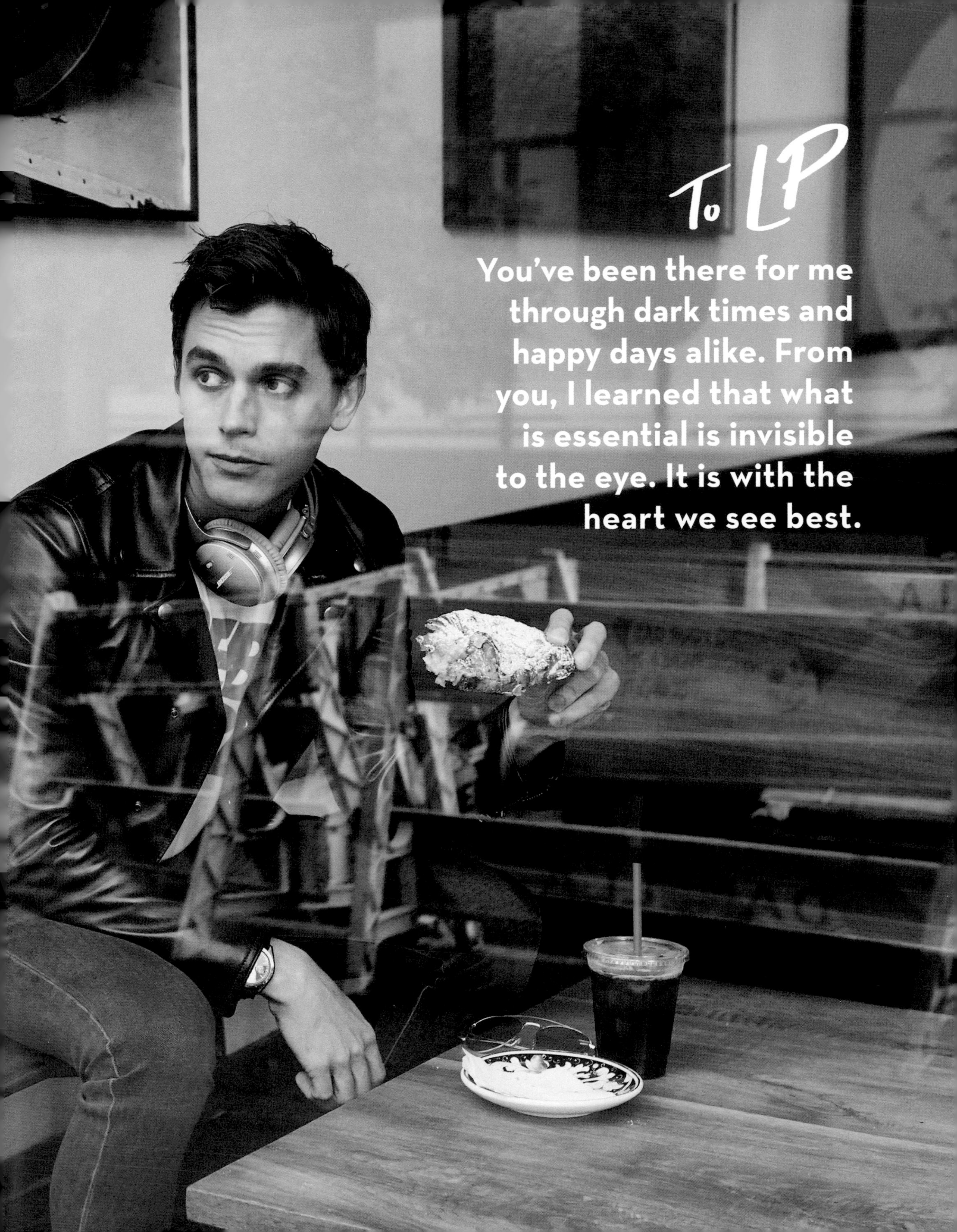

To LP

You've been there for me through dark times and happy days alike. From you, I learned that what is essential is invisible to the eye. It is with the heart we see best.

Acknowledgments

I know very well that "it takes a village," and I'm so very grateful to have one. Writing this book connected me with a group of incredibly talented women and men, and reconnected me with Polish family members and other loved ones. It also turned out to be a great adventure in digging deep into my food memories and collaborating with like-minded people who express their love through the sharing of food.

To my dear coauthor, Mindy Fox, I cannot believe how lucky I am to have met you. Your love and respect for food is admirable, and your attention to the minutest of details, along with endless hours of work on recipes and words, have made this book what it is. Your gentle nature and patience encouraged me to trust my own voice. I'm honored that you agreed to collaborate with me and excited for more opportunities to come. Also, since my dad sent you his Vermont maple syrup, I'm pretty sure that means you're part of the family now, so yeah . . .

My editor, the culinary world's own Grace Coddington, Rux Martin. I admire your honesty and directness, which come with equal amounts of heart, patience, and invaluable guidance. I hope that with this book I've made you proud.

Ted Allen and Barry Rice, my friends, former employers, and forever mentors. Knowing you has helped me expand my food, design, and vintage furniture know-how, and hone my basic human skills, like drafting e-mails and calendaring. Your respective passions gave me the confidence to pursue my own.

To my family, including my parents, Janusz and Janina; my sisters, Karolina and Aleksandra; my aunties, Magda S, Magda J, and Leslie; Uncle Andy; and Cousin Maïa. Working on both Polish and family-inspired recipes for this book allowed me to revisit my childhood and heritage and renewed my appreciation and respect for both of those things. I am a proud Polish-Canadian-American because of each and every one of you.

To Joey, Minette, Jim, Bess, and Joe. Our years together gave me what I'd been searching for my whole life: a family to cook for. You gave me your hearts and your kitchens so I could feel safe in giving you back my love and my food. Many of the recipes in this book were tested on you before the crazy life I have now. Joey, you were my number-one supporter in life and work, and I will never forget that.

Mindy and I would like to thank Beth Barden and Jennifer Ophir, our uber-talented recipe testers. We cherish your honesty, feedback, and skill in the kitchen. Beth, you made Kansas City feel like home.

Paul Brissman, your beautiful food photography, journalistic approach to lifestyle photos, and love for New York and all of its side streets took this book to another level.

Food stylist Lisa Homa and prop stylist Kristine Trevino, thank you for your dedication and stunning work.

Book designer Laura Palese, thank you for putting it all together and in such a unique and gorgeous way.

Melissa Lotfy, Jamie Selzer, Judith Sutton, Sarah Kwak, Crystal Paquette, and Jacinta Monniere, thank you for brightening all the corners of this book.

Glam and styling squad, Nina Soriano and Matty Bidgoli, I'm so sorry I distracted you endlessly while you tried to do your jobs. You're the real deal (and fun to distract).

Alex Kovacs, Jason Weinberg, and Jamieson Baker at Untitled Entertainment. Alex's logistical aptitude is what allowed me to write this book while filming in Kansas City and to make my flights back to New York to attend photo shoots.

My agents, David Larabell and Ben Levine at CAA. After moving to New York and later attending meetings at your offices with my then-boss, Ted Allen, I only dreamed of one day being represented by such a supportive team. I am a damn lucky guy.

To the entire team at Scout Productions, David Collins, Michael Williams, Rob Eric, and Joel Chiodi; the fabulous support at ITV from Ally Capriotti Grant, Jordy Hochman, Danielle Gervais, Gretchen Palek, Beyhan Oguz, David George, Adam Sher, and David Eilenberg; Jenn Levy and the team at Netflix; and executive producers Jen Lane and Rachelle Mendez and the crew on- and off-set at *Queer Eye*, who foster a warm and collaborative working environment.

To Hanya Yanagihara, for your friendship and support; Klaus Biesenbach, confidant and mentor, for teaching me the many benefits that come from making mistakes; PJ Vogt, for encouraging me to pursue multiple passions; and Christian Coulson, for reminding me to be gentle with myself.

To Reema Sampat, my best friend, confidant, hero, mother to my goddaughter Mara, inspiration for many recipes, and biggest cheerleader.

And last but far from least, my *Queer Eye* brothers, Bobby Berk, Karamo Brown, Tanny France, and Jonathan Van Ness, for being beloved friends, honest taste testers, and the supportive backbone in all of my endeavors.

—Antoni Porowski

Enormous gratitude to Antoni Porowski: Bringing this book to life with you was an honor and a dream adventure—inspiring, enlightening, and so much fun at every turn. Thank you for trusting me as a partner; for sharing your boundless passion, culinary prowess, and smarts; and for being the incredibly loving and delightful person that you are. You had me at Boursin and frozen peas. I can't wait to see what's next. I am also deeply grateful to my agent, Sarah Smith, at David Black Agency; our editor, Rux Martin; my husband, Steve Hoffman, and our beloved canine companion, Jasper; Neil, Phyllis, and Jason Fox; Ellen Rudley; all the Hoffmans, especially caramel-code-cracker extraordinaire Abbi Hoffman; my extended Northeast, Midwest, and Southern families; and the many friends and colleagues who continue to cheer me on.

—Mindy Fox

Foreword

In the steamy summer of 2003, *Queer Eye* was an immediate hit for Bravo that ran for ninety-nine or a hundred episodes, depending on whom you ask. In that run, it made a lasting impact on the culture.

It got us onto the covers of magazines, *Ellen*, *Oprah*, the *Tonight Show* (twice), and the morning talk shows (I still chuckle at how hard it was for Matt Lauer to wrap his mouth around the word "queer"). There were *New Yorker* cartoons, an appearance in the comic strip *Blondie*, and satellite media tours with radio and TV all over the country.

Queer Eye was innovative: the first national television show with an entirely out, gay cast. The first program to smash together gay and straight cultures, employing real people as themselves and letting the chips fall. It was funny as hell (and you should have heard the funny stuff that wasn't airable—actually, no, you shouldn't have). It was one of the very few makeover shows with a truly talented interior designer.

And it was an inspiration to so many LGBTQ kids and adults. They told us so, thousands of times—still do today. That is the thing about *Queer Eye* that mattered most—and matters still. In millions of homes both liberal and conservative, *Queer Eye* showed—and shows again—the world that gay and straight folks could get along fine; that gays could be successful, leaders, teachers, your friends, not just tolerated, not just accepted, but welcomed and admired. Loved, even. We won an Emmy Award. (Am I steamed that the new version won *three* of them? HELLS, YES! Actually, not really.) One of us OG QEs, whose name I'll

TRIBECA EAST HISTORIC DISTRICT
LISPENARD ST
ONE WAY
ONE WAY
PRADA
GUCCI
CANAL FURNITURE
402 BROADWAY TEL: 925-5343
KAIZEN
WALKER ST
CAUTION
CUIDADO
NO HOUSEHOLD TRASH
NO BUSINESS TRASH
$100 FINE
GANZ!

What makes him special is the key ingredient that makes *Queer Eye* special: heart.

keep to myself, uses his statuette as a toilet-paper holder at his lake house; a roll fits perfectly on her upswept wings. Keepin' it real, yo.

I met Antoni at a signing for my second cookbook, and we hit it off. As it happened, my husband, Barry Rice, and I needed an assistant, both at home and at Barry's designer furniture business, Full Circle Modern. Antoni needed a job flexible enough that he could go to auditions. It was a perfect fit. He worked for us for more than three years, and he showed himself a *very* quick study in marketing, furniture craftsmanship, and interior design. And the food! I loved it every time Antoni made his New-Style Polish Hunter's Stew. I will never forget how great it was to have him in the house making lunches for us, how he connected us with bartenders for special events, how creative he got helping us prep for parties. Antoni is a details guy, with endless imagination and an arsenal of techniques. And BTW, there was rarely an avocado in sight!

When he told me he wanted to make a go for *Queer Eye*, I texted his CV and headshot to David Collins, the cocreator of the show. His reply: "Yowza!" Of course, it was up to Antoni to prove himself in person. Over the course of weeks of auditions and callbacks—and now, episode after episode—he did.

He proves himself again with this book: a veritable culinary travelogue, with nods to his family's Canadian roots, and detours to every place from Lyon to Athens to Melbourne. Tuck into Warm Herbed Olives with Marcona Almonds. Take on a lesson in building the perfect cheese platter, inspired by the ones Antoni's dad made every Friday evening. Get seriously luxurious with Herbed Lobster and Saffron Dip. Everybody's into cauliflower steaks—but you haven't had Antoni's, with turmeric and crunchy almonds. Roasted Sweet Potato Fries with Chimichurri—why didn't I think of that? Make a Farro Bowl with Sweet Potatoes, Arugula, and Chicken, and you've got lunch ready for a whole work week (my favorite thing that Antoni taught me). Finish things off with Vanilla Pots de Crème with Mango Coulis or a Raspberry Mousse Dome—you're off to a great start!

Antoni's culinary skills are prodigious, but what makes him special is the key ingredient that makes *Queer Eye* special: heart. The best *QE*s were—and are—the ones where you can feel the featured Heroes showing a little resistance at first, but then watch them realize how profound it is to have five caring people come into your life and work hard to make your life better. The tears are real. And Antoni's desire to share his vision for a brighter, yummier world doesn't come from books and practice—it comes from inside. You'll feel it when you start your first dish in this book, carefully and patiently guided. You'll *really* feel it when you take your first bite.

—Ted Allen

Contents

Introduction

Have you ever felt your face flush, your insides turn manic, and your sense of gravity vanish all at once? That's how it was for me one unusually warm March day in 2017 when my phone buzzed and the name Rob Eric, Emmy-winning television producer and co-creator of *Queer Eye*, appeared on the screen.

I was working as a curator and director at High Style Deco—a high-end art deco and mid-century modern gallery in New York City's Chelsea neighborhood—and moments away from closing the sale of a solid brass sideboard once owned by Andy Warhol. Politely excusing myself from my client, I walked in what felt like slow motion to a quiet corner of the room.

Rob spoke for a minute or two. I felt my eyes well up and my voice crack. I swallowed, took a moment to catch my breath, and thanked him about fourteen times, the words "We'd love for you to be part of the show" echoing in my head. I hung up and immediately called my partner at the time, Joey. "Congratulations!" he said. "You did it."

Joey rushed over after work and met me at the gallery. Riding the subway from Manhattan to our apartment in Brooklyn that night, we just stared at each other, giggling and smiling stupidly. Was this all really happening? At home, I sat down on the edge of our bed, feeling the mix of elation and relief that comes from waiting for weeks, sometimes months, to hear back about a part. I was five years out of acting school and had been on countless auditions, landing a few roles here and there, but nothing like this.

ENTER, STAGE LEFT: Crippling self-doubt.

Was I a total imposter?

LOVE YOU SO BAD
LOVE YOU SO BAD
LOVE YOU SO BAD
LOVE YOU SO BAD
LOVE YOU SO BAD
LOVE YOU SO BAD
LOVE YOU SO BAD
LOVE YOU SO BAD
OVE YOU SO BAD
4TH
ORK

For one, I questioned whether I was gay enough to be on a show called *Queer Eye*. Yes, I was living with a man I dearly loved. But I had never come out as gay, never felt polarized at one end of the sexuality spectrum, never felt entirely sure whether I'd live forever as a gay man or fall in love and spend my life with a woman.

And, really, was I enough of a food guy? Many of the contenders I'd been up against for the role of *Queer Eye* "food and wine expert" had longtime careers as chefs, food-industry people, and food personalities. Sure, I had worked in restaurants and been a private chef, waded into TV food territory by auditioning for the part of host for *Chopped Canada*, and taped a short *Tasting Table* video or two, but my food passion felt more personal than professional. I saw myself as an aspiring actor, my work in the food business as a means to an end. It would be a full season of working on *Queer Eye* before I realized the track was one I'd been on all my life.

ENTER, STAGE LEFT: Crippling self-doubt. Was I a total imposter?

GROWING UP POLISH

I was born and raised in Montreal. My parents, both Polish, came from upper-middle-class families. My father had been raised in Montreal (his parents having fled Poland during World War II), but my mother had lived in Poland until her early twenties, when she met and married my dad. Both were well educated and had fairly broad palates, but they also clung tightly to the food traditions of their Polish heritage.

Following the path of my sisters, Karolina and Aleksandra (my elders by fifteen and nine years), I went to Ecole Saint-Laurent, a French school with a student body made up of kids from Indian, Eastern European, Portuguese, Iranian, Lebanese, Egyptian, Chinese, and Vietnamese families. My favorite event of the year was Le Buffet des Nations (The Buffet of Nations), which took place in the school gym. Each family brought a dish from their country and, sharing them, we learned about the faraway places our parents had come from. My Portuguese-Iranian friend Andrew Shahidi's parents brought *tahdig*, a delicious rice dish with a golden, crispy panfried bottom. There were tagines and egg rolls and curries. My mom made a version of a Polish classic called *krokiety*, thin rolled crepes

When Saturday school let out, we'd buy little plum jam–filled doughnuts, called *pączki*, from Pâtisserie Wawel on Rue Sherbrooke, then head to Wayne's Deli—a Polish grocery named for a Canadian man who had married a woman from the motherland and turned his obsession with the food of her country into a roaring business.

Alongside the cheeses were carefully considered pairings like Champagne grapes, fresh figs, thinly sliced Anjou pears, and roasted Marcona almonds, along with three kinds of bread, which often included the famous baguette trente-six heures.

stuffed with meat or mushrooms, dipped in egg, rolled in bread crumbs, and fried in butter. She'd fancy hers up with handpicked morels and chanterelles and a Cognac-cream sauce.

On Saturdays I went to Polish school, where I learned history, language, spelling, and dictation and practiced Catholic prayer. Mrs. Siwikowa, the principal and my teacher, wore the same beehive hairstyle and triangular glasses she had when my dad was her student more than three decades earlier.

When Saturday school let out, we'd buy little plum jam–filled doughnuts, called *pączki,* from Pâtisserie Wawel on Rue Sherbrooke, then head to Wayne's Deli—a Polish grocery named for a Canadian man who had married a woman from the motherland and turned his obsession with the food of her country into a roaring business. There we'd get fresh handmade pierogies, house-smoked kielbasa, Polish ham, headcheese, sauerkraut, and pastries, plus little treats like *krówki* (milky fudge candies) and Prince Polo Bars (the Polish version of Kit Kats).

At home my mom put together the big Saturday spread. She crisped up slices of kielbasa in a skillet and arranged them on a platter with sauerkraut and a crock of hot Polish mustard. My father, who was in charge of anything that was put on bread, spread slices of fresh rye with cold butter, then layered on sliced ham, a smear of Poland's beloved Kielecki mayonnaise, and razor-thin slices of very dill-y pickles that came from the barrel at the deli.

For culinary inspiration outside her Polish repertoire, my mom turned to classics like beef Stroganoff, which she made often during the cold Montreal winters. My parents went sailing in the British Virgin Islands every December, and my mom came back with recipes like mango-wrapped roast salmon topped with bubbling charred Brie from chic waterfront restaurants where they'd eaten.

I never cooked with my mother; she didn't like anyone helping her in the kitchen. But she was happy to let me sit with a little snack at the other end of the island and watch. Just before a dish was ready, she'd let me weigh in on any final salt and pepper adjustments. I loved tasting and being part of it all.

QUÉBÉCOIS SUMMERS AND DINNER PARTIES AT FOURTEEN

My father wasn't a cook, but he loved food. On Friday nights, he put together his famous cheese board. There were always at least four or five varieties, including a rich triple-cream selection, like Délice de Bourgogne, and one real stinker (often an Epoisses or Valdeón) that had to be held under a glass cloche lest its aroma become offensive. We almost always had our very favorite, Riopelle de l'Isle, a buttery soft-ripened type from Quebec, named after the famous Québécois abstract expressionist artist Jean-Paul Riopelle. Alongside the cheeses were carefully considered pairings like Champagne grapes, fresh figs, thinly sliced Anjou pears, and roasted Marcona almonds, along with three kinds of bread, which often included the famous baguette trente-six heures (the dough was fermented for thirty-six hours before baking) from a bakery called Au Pain d'Oré.

It was during summers with my Aunt Magda J that I first had the chance to get into the kitchen. She and Uncle Stefan had a big log cabin in the historic village of Knowlton, in Quebec. Situated on acres of rolling hills with a magical wooded perimeter, it was the place where our relatives and close family friends and their kids all convened. We played by the lake and went horseback riding nearby. It was our own special summer camp.

Along with all the fun, everyone had to sign up for a task. My favorite was being in the kitchen, where I helped cook, set the table, and do the dishes. My cousin Maïa let me help her measure the ingredients and stir together the dough for her lemon bars. I came to appreciate the whole process of serving a meal, and I loved the collaborative nature and inclusivity of working as a team in the kitchen.

Around the same time, my sister Aleks signed up for a subscription to *Martha Stewart Living*. Aleks would re-create dishes from the magazine, and she was drawn to the visual aspects of both the food and tabletop decor. I was curious about how the recipes worked. Aleks and I didn't get along very well during those years, but the magazine showed us that we shared a common passion, and it sparked my interest in entertaining.

I didn't realize it at the time, but I longed for family.

When I finished elementary school, my father took a job in West Virginia, since it was typical at the time for Canadian doctors to head south for better work opportunities. I went with him and my mom, while my sisters stayed behind in our house in Montreal. My father worked around the clock, including nights and weekends, and my mother split her time between the States and Canada, which often left me alone. I didn't realize it at the time, but I longed for family.

At fourteen, I began hosting dinner parties for my friends. Cooking for and sharing food with people gave me the comfort of the family experience I needed. My signature dish was warm roasted garlic spread onto torn pieces of baguette and served with nuggets of Parmesan cheese. I made sure to have the garlic finishing up in the oven when my friends arrived, so the warmth and fragrance would welcome them. The menu continued with dishes like grilled chicken that had been marinated in a raspberry barbecue sauce, which I served with fresh raspberries on the side. I piled slices of grilled zucchini and bell peppers onto a big platter and topped them with fresh oregano and a drizzle of olive oil and red wine vinegar. When I was feeding just myself, I folded grated Parm and frozen peas into boxed mac and cheese.

RESTAURANT SHIFTS AND HANGOVER CURES

I went back to Montreal for prep school when I was seventeen and got my first job working in a supper club called Buonanotte, where I was a busboy and runner. While I was there, I met and became friends with Chuck Hughes and Tim Rozon, then-unknowns who later became successful in their respective careers as chef and actor, along with my pals Kyle Marshall Nares and Andy Weinman. Andy was from Australia, and he made a snack for us of toasted white bread spread with margarine and Vegemite and topped with Swiss cheese. He deemed it his hangover cure, which, I have to say, worked quite well. I topped it with a crispy egg one morning to make it a more complete breakfast. I still make a variation of that egg-toast today (page 162).

At Concordia University, I took acting classes on the side while studying psychology and art history, and I spent my weekends waiting tables at a classic Polish restaurant, Stash Café. Stash was owned by my Auntie Ewa at the time, and working there was a family tradition. My dad had put in his hours when he was in college; Auntie Magda and her three daughters, Olga, Marta, and Maïa, had all been employees, and so had both of my sisters when they were in school. Located in a historic seventeenth-century building on a cobblestone street in the heart of the city's Old Port, it's a magical little place, dimly lit with a warm glow from red-shaded lamps that hang from the rough-hewn wood-beamed ceiling. There are church pews for seats and art deco–style film and theater prints by the Polish painter Tamara de Lempicka. Vodka is kept in a dedicated freezer. (Today Stash is one of the few remaining Polish restaurants in Montreal.)

I always showed up for my lunch shift horribly hungover. A rickety staircase led to the basement prep area, where a group of Polish grandmothers made pierogies, cooked the beets for the borscht and chlodnik, rolled krokiety, stirred big pots of bigos stew, pounded pork chops, shaved cabbage, and cut carrots into the shape of flowers that they dyed red with beet juice and served with a sprig of parsley to mimic a rose. They were stocky women, with ankles that matched the size of their hefty calves. As tough on us waiters as they were during service, they made sure we started and ended our shifts with full bellies. Pani (Lady) Marysia always greeted me when I arrived and offered me a steaming bowl of *zurek* (a hearty sausage and vegetable soup) topped with an extra helping of hard-boiled eggs and a double or triple spoonful of sour cream. I would go upstairs, devour it, and feel human again.

Chuck Hughes opened his restaurant Garde Manger in 2006, and I left Stash to work there as a waiter as part of the opening crew. The place was an instant success. The market-driven menu changed daily. I learned about king eryngii (aka king oyster) mushrooms, which Chuck served in a gratin with raclette cheese and fresh herbs, and beluga lentils, which he piled onto toasted crusty bread with oven-roasted tomatoes and celery leaves. It was an exhilarating place to work.

I always showed up for my lunch shift horribly hungover. A rickety staircase led to the basement prep area, where a group of Polish grandmothers made pierogies, cooked the beets for the borscht and chlodnik, rolled krokiety, stirred big pots of bigos stew, pounded pork chops, shaved cabbage, and cut carrots into the shape of flowers that they dyed red with beet juice and served with a sprig of parsley to mimic a rose. They were stocky women, with ankles that matched the size of their hefty calves.

A SHOW CALLED *QUEER EYE*

About a year later, I landed a spot as a student at The Neighborhood Playhouse in New York City, where the revered instructor Sanford Meisner had trained stars like Robert Duvall and Mary Steenburgen. Just before graduating, I fell in love with Joey Krietemeyer, who would be my partner and family for the next seven years. Joey's parents, Minette and Jim, had just moved from the Midwest to New York to be closer to him and his sister, Bess, who both lived in the Clinton Hill neighborhood of Brooklyn. I loved his family from the get-go, and we began a tradition of having dinner together on Sundays.

All week long, I looked forward to cooking for my new family, planning meals that echoed the American comfort foods that Joey and Bess grew up eating and that I spun with a contemporary twist. Things like cheesy turkey meatloaf flavored with fresh herbs (page 222) and mac and cheese with peas (page 146), but also healthy dishes like Roasted Carrots with Carrot-Top Pesto (page 94), Cauliflower "Rice" with Parmigiano (page 96), and Grilled Peach and Tomato Salad (page 81).

By that time, I was tired of waiting tables and working late nights. I had graduated from The Playhouse and I was still taking acting workshops and auditioning, but I was trying to figure out what I would do next to pay the bills. My friend PJ Vogt had long encouraged me to pursue my passion for food, and one day he mentioned that a guy named Ted Allen—the OG food and wine expert on the original *Queer Eye* and now host of the food show *Chopped*—had just come out with a cookbook and was signing books at Greenlight Bookstore that night.

Joey came with me to the event, and we struck up a conversation with Ted and discovered we were neighbors. Ted was headed to a community wine-tasting event where he'd meet up with his husband, Barry Rice. He invited us along. It wasn't long before the four of us became close friends. Ted and Barry were looking to hire someone to help them with administrative tasks and research for a new business. Knowing I was on the hunt for work, they offered me the job. The hours were flexible, which meant I could dip out to auditions at a moment's notice. It was perfect.

FOOD MARKET INC. 劉氏食品公
CASHIER

Barry had an extensive mid-century modern furniture collection and was considering starting a gallery, so I assisted by documenting his existing pieces, purchasing new ones from auction, and finding high-end upholsterers, caners, and glassworkers. I organized Ted's press engagements and coordinated his busy calendar. All the while, I was learning about production schedules, meeting people in the food world, writing about food, and helping Ted with his research for public speaking events on food and nutrition. Without realizing it, I was preparing for *Queer Eye*.

In the coming pages, you'll find a mix of food that mirrors my life's path as well as my own discoveries. Soups and stews like zurek (page 124), bigos (page 137), and chlodnik (page 117)—recipes that my parents brought from Poland to North America—keep me connected to my roots. Alsatian Tarts (page 68) and Spicy Fennel Frico (page 65) are some of the snacks I lean on when I invite friends over for a casual party, while I turn to healthy dishes like Carrot Ribbon Salad with Ginger, Parsley, and Dates (page 86) and Tangy Beluga Lentils (page 110) for energy during the workweek.

I hope the recipes in this book bring joy to your kitchen and inspire you to discover the dishes that have shaped you. Nothing would make me prouder or happier.

MY TOP TEN CULINARY MANTRAS

1

Buy the best ingredients you can get. Pared-down dishes made with high-quality ingredients are the ones that taste the best and are the most satisfying to make.

2

Don't put too much pressure on yourself when you're entertaining. Lean on snacks that can be prepared ahead, like Warm Herbed Olives with Marcona Almonds (page 38), Cheesy Lemon-Rosemary Artichoke Dip (page 53), or a cheese platter (page 49).

3

Stock a good pantry. Items like good olive oil, nuts, quick-cooking grains, and canned beans can help you put together a variety of dishes in a flash.

4

Cheese and nuts do wonders in adding depth of flavor and texture to all sorts of dishes, especially snacks, salads, and vegetables.

5

A collection of little veg plates, like the Asparagus with Oozy Eggs (page 88), Duck Fat–Roasted Potato Salad with Mustardy Sauce (page 84), and Summer Corn with Chorizo and Cilantro (page 100), can be put together to make a complete lunch or dinner.

6

Dessert can be as simple as a stack of Ginger-Cardamom Cowboy Cookies (page 240) or a plate of watermelon, ginger, and mint (page 255).

7

Retro is fun, especially when it's meaningful to you. Case in point: my mom's Raspberry Mousse Dome (page 252).

8

Any hangover, no matter how vicious, can be soothed with a bowl of hot zurek (page 124).

9

French omelettes (page 164) **are romantic.**

10

Frozen peas for president.

APPS AND SNACKS

The Perfect Bite

Medjool Dates with Blue Cheese, Marcona Almonds + Prosciutto

Serves 4 to 6

This simple hors d'oeuvre represents how I approach every dish I make, by seeking to achieve a balance of flavors. The little nugget first hits the lips with salt and a bit of fat, followed by sweet and sticky, then sharp and funky, and finally a welcoming crunch to finish it off. Medjool dates are known for their large size and caramel-like sweetness, attributes that make them perfect for this recipe. I like Marcona almonds here, because of their sweet, buttery flavor, but any good-quality roasted salted almonds will do.

24 Medjool dates, preferably pitted

¼ pound thinly sliced prosciutto

3 ounces blue cheese

24 roasted salted almonds, preferably Marcona

Heat the oven to 375°F, with a rack in the middle. Line a baking sheet with parchment paper.

If the dates are not already pitted, make an incision down the side of each one and remove the pits.

Cut or tear the slices of prosciutto lengthwise into strips about 1¼ inches wide. If you don't wind up with a total of 24 strips, cut a few in half to make up the difference.

Listening to Miles Davis's *Kind of Blue*, stuff each date with a nub (about ½ teaspoon) of blue cheese and an almond. Gently press to close up the opening, then wrap the dates in the prosciutto strips. Place the dates on the baking sheet, cut side up so that the cheese doesn't all ooze out.

Bake the dates until warm and slightly bubbling, 7 to 10 minutes. Remove from the oven and let cool for a few minutes before serving. These are magical warm but totally acceptable at room temp.

Tip With its creamy semisoft texture and funky but not-too-intense flavor, Saint Agur, which melts like a champ, is my preferred blue for this dish. That said, there really is no wrong blue cheese option here. Cambozola, a Brie-style blue, offers a luxe creaminess and milder flavor, while sharp Stilton gives the sweetness of the dates a more robust flavor to bump up against. A crumbly Danish variety wouldn't be the end of the world, especially if you prefer milder blues, and, since it's a drier cheese, it makes assembly a bit less messy.

Warm Herbed Olives

with Marcona Almonds

Serves 4 to 6

I first had these warm olives at Le Dominion, my favorite hotel in Quebec City. Since then, I've made them a zillion times, varying the herbs and sometimes, as here, tossing in Marcona almonds, which add a sweet, toasty flavor and crunch. These are the perfect snack, enjoyed on their own or with a baguette and cheese. Any olive variety you like works well, but a mix is especially attractive.

3/4 pound (about 2 1/2 cups) mixed unseasoned olives (with or without pits), such as Castelvetrano, oil-cured Moroccan, and Kalamata, drained

1/2 cup (2 ounces) roasted salted Marcona almonds

1/4 cup extra-virgin olive oil

1 tablespoon red wine vinegar

1 1/2 teaspoons finely chopped fresh rosemary, plus 1 sprig, cut into 2-inch lengths

1 1/2 teaspoons finely chopped fresh thyme, plus 1 sprig, cut into 2-inch lengths

In a medium saucepan, combine the olives, almonds, oil, vinegar, and chopped rosemary and thyme and heat over medium heat, stirring occasionally, until the olives are warm and fragrant, 4 to 5 minutes. Remove from the heat.

Stir in the herb sprigs, then transfer to a serving bowl. Serve warm or at room temperature.

Tip Although pitted olives always seem appealing at the market, I usually go for pits-in. Pitted olives tend to absorb more brine than their intact counterparts, and the brine adds extra salt, which can overwhelm the complex fruity notes and turn the flesh mushy or pasty.

Reema's Masala Nuts

Makes about 5 cups

I smile whenever I make this recipe, not only because it's completely addictive, but also because it makes me think of my very best friend, Reema Sampat, who shared it during season two of *Queer Eye* when I wanted a simple Indian-inspired, flavor-bomb snack. Jason (the Burning Man guy) was a big fan of both peanuts and Indian cuisine, so I introduced him to the vibrant, robust flavors that typify a lot of Indian street food and taught him how to take his favorite snack to another level. Browning the nuts in a little oil before tossing them with the spices crisps them and helps the spices adhere.

---

2 cups coarsely chopped red onions

2 teaspoons extra-virgin olive oil

1 (16-ounce) jar roasted unsalted peanuts (3⅓ cups)

2¼ teaspoons ground turmeric

½ teaspoon cayenne pepper

1 packed tablespoon grated lime zest

⅓ cup fresh lime juice (from 2 to 3 large limes)

1¾ teaspoons kosher salt

2 cups coarsely chopped fresh cilantro leaves and tender stems

Place the onions in a medium bowl, add a few ice cubes, and cover with very cold water. Set aside. (Soaking the onions removes a bit of the sharp bite. If you like intense, as my Reema does, skip this step.)

In a very large (12-inch) nonstick or stainless-steel skillet, heat the oil over medium-high heat. Add the nuts, reduce the heat to medium-low, and cook, stirring frequently and keeping an eye on your pan (you can't undo burnt nuts), until the nuts are about two shades darker and have a deeply roasty fragrance, 15 to 20 minutes. (The crunchier and darker brown, the better.)

Clear a space in the center of your pan and add the turmeric and cayenne to the cleared space. Toast the spices, undisturbed, until fragrant, about 1 minute, then quickly but carefully add the lime zest, lime juice (the pan will steam a bit), and salt and stir everything together to coat the peanuts with the spices. Remove the pan from the heat, transfer the spiced nuts to a serving bowl, and let cool for 5 to 10 minutes.

Drain the onions and pat dry with a clean dishtowel. Add the onions and cilantro to the nuts and toss to combine. Serve with a spoon! No need for a finger orgy in the serving dish.

Two Favorite Street Snacks

I love these two deliciously fresh street snacks, from different corners of the world. I learned about the jicama version from one of my besties, Ariadna. In Mexico, peeled jicama is cut into sticks, drenched in lime juice, seasoned with salt and chili powder or Tajín Clásico (a popular seasoning made with dried chile peppers, salt, and dehydrated lime juice), and enjoyed as a crunchy snack. The mango version, visually similar, is a Malaysian one that I discovered during my time as a waiter at Fatty Crab in New York City. Its flavor plays off a similar trifecta of tangy, spicy, and subtly sweet seasonings. This duo exemplifies the universality of certain flavor profiles, whether you're in Mexico or Malaysia. There's something comforting and philosophical there, I believe.

Jicama with Lime and Tajín

Serves 4

1 baseball-sized jicama (about 1½ pounds)

Grated zest and juice of 1 large lime

2 teaspoons Tajín Clásico seasoning (see Tip)

Flaky sea salt, such as Maldon

Peel the jicama with a sharp vegetable peeler, then slice it into ½-inch-thick sticks. In a large bowl, toss together the jicama, lime zest and juice, Tajín, and a generous pinch of flaky salt. Arrange on a large platter and serve.

If you can't find Tajín Clásico, Mrs. Dash Fiesta Lime seasoning blend or any basic chili powder makes a great substitute. If you go with one that is salt-free, you'll want to add salt to taste.

Green Mango with Chili-Sugar-Salt

Serves 4 to 6

1 tablespoon sugar

1 teaspoon chili powder

½ teaspoon cayenne pepper

¼ teaspoon kosher salt

2 green (unripe) mangoes, peeled, pitted, and cut into ½-inch-thick sticks

Mix together the sugar and spices in a small serving bowl. Arrange the mango sticks on a large platter and serve with the spice mixture for dipping.

Green (or underripe) mangoes are firmer and more tart than the ripe orange-red ones. They're great in salads and this snack. To cut them, first remove the skin with a sharp veg peeler, then cut a small piece from the bottom (non-stem) end to create a flat base so you can stand the mango upright. With a chef's knife, starting about ½ inch to the right of the center, so you don't hit the pit, cut down the length of the fruit to remove the flesh in one piece. Repeat on the other side of the pit. Set the pit piece aside. Lay one piece of the cut flesh on your cutting board and cut lengthwise into ½-inch-wide pieces, then cut each piece lengthwise into irregular-shaped sticks. Repeat with the second cut piece. Now cut the flesh from the pit; these pieces will be very irregular, but they taste just as good.

1990s Porowski Goat Cheese Canapés

Makes 18 canapés

These were served at nine out of ten of the parties my parents threw before any holiday or event. I would watch my mother and middle sister, Aleks (who loved to do anything decorative), assemble each canapé with meticulous precision. Luckily, even with a lactose intolerance, I was able to eat goat cheese with abandon, so these were a savior for me in the face of the many other cheesy delights I couldn't enjoy at the time. (Yeah, I fought it out of me.) I love the texture and added flavor that a soft fresh goat cheese with a rind lends to these snacks (an option you'll find at cheese markets or in supermarkets with a good selection), but you can also use the more common rind-less variety.

Tip For cheese slices that won't stick to your knife, don't use a knife! Instead, use a piece of unflavored dental floss. Hold it taut with one end in each of your hands and press straight down through the log to make a clean, even cut. (You can use the same trick to cut logs of cookie dough.)

1 baguette

1 (10.5-ounce) log goat cheese (see headnote)

12 oil-packed sun-dried tomatoes, each sliced lengthwise into 3 thin strips, plus 3 tablespoons oil from the jar

¼ cup pine nuts

6 to 8 fresh basil leaves

Heat the oven to 400°F, with a rack in the upper third.

Cut eighteen ½-inch-thick slices from the baguette and arrange on a baking sheet.

Cut the goat cheese into 18 rounds. Arrange the cheese on top of the bread, then top each piece with 2 strips of sun-dried tomato arranged in an X. Top the canapés with the pine nuts and drizzle with the sun-dried tomato oil.

Bake until the pine nuts are golden and the cheese is beginning to melt, 6 to 8 minutes.

Meanwhile, stack the basil leaves in a neat pile, tightly roll them up lengthwise, and, using a sharp chef's knife, cut the roll crosswise into thin ribbons. (This cut is called a chiffonade, if you want to impress anyone creeping on your knife skills as you do it.)

Remove the canapés from the oven and transfer to a serving platter. Top with the basil. Serve hot.

Pickled Herring Tartines

with Tart Apple + Shaved Radishes

Makes 6 tartines or 24 canapés

Traditionally served at our very Polish Christmas Eve, when we'd have platters piled high with herring and all sorts of accompaniments to create our own custom plates, this tartine recalls the combination of flavors that my oldest sister, Karolina, and I love. Bites of thinly sliced peppery radish and sweet-tart green apple are the perfect contrast to the salty tang of pickled herring, and a dollop of sour cream and chopped dill round it all out. Delicious as tartines—breads or toasts topped with a few ingredients and served open-faced—these also make a delightful hors d'oeuvre when cut into bite-sized canapés.

---

6 slices (about ¼-inch-thick) dense Baltic rye, kamut, or spelt bread, lightly toasted and cooled

5 tablespoons unsalted butter, slightly softened

Flaky sea salt, such as Maldon

1 small Granny Smith apple, halved, cored, and thinly sliced

1 (12-ounce) jar pickled herring in wine sauce, drained, any pickled onions reserved

4 small radishes, very thinly sliced

1 small shallot, thinly sliced

Heaping ⅓ cup full-fat sour cream

2 tablespoons coarsely chopped fresh dill

Coarsely ground black pepper

Spread the toasts with the butter. Sprinkle each with a pinch of flaky salt, then fan apple slices on top. Top each tartine with some herring, a few radish slices, some shallot, and some reserved pickled onions, if you have them, then dollop with about 1 tablespoon of the sour cream. For canapés, cut each tartine into 4 pieces. Top with the dill and pepper and serve.

Tips

If you have a mandoline slicer, use it to slice the radishes into paper-thin rounds.

If you're serving drinks with these tartines, go for an icy chilled vodka, as my family would do. (Store your vodka in the freezer, always. It'll keep your cocktails cooler longer.) Wine does not pair well with pickled herring; it gives an unpleasant metallic aftertaste.

Slow-Roasted Garlic

WITH PARMIGIANO-REGGIANO NUGGETS + HONEY

Serves 4 to 6

Slow-roasted garlic is my personal version of cookies baking in the oven: Fragrant wafts of warmth and familiarity greet your guests as they enter your home. While you can blitz the deeply toasty roasted cloves into salad dressings, marinades, mojo sauces, and more, this dish makes them star of the show, simply pairing them with good bread, high-quality cheese, and a light drizzle of sweet, sticky honey. Set it out at your next dinner party and let guests build their own bites.

1/2 pound whole garlic heads (3 to 4, depending on size)

About 1 1/2 tablespoons extra-virgin olive oil

Kosher salt

A 1/2-pound wedge of aged Parmigiano-Reggiano

1 baguette

1/3 cup clover honey (or your favorite unflavored variety) for drizzling

Heat the oven to 375°F, with a rack in the middle.

Cut off the top ¼ to ½ inch from each garlic head, exposing the cloves. One at a time, place each head in the center of a sheet of foil large enough to enclose it, drizzle with 1½ teaspoons of the oil, and sprinkle with a generous pinch of salt. Wrap the head fairly tightly in the foil.

Place the packets directly on the middle oven rack and roast until the cloves are dark brown and as soft as butter, 40 to 50 minutes. Remove the packets from the oven and let cool for 5 to 7 minutes, then unwrap.

To serve, set the heads of roasted garlic on a wooden cutting board or serving platter. Arrange your block of Parmigiano, a paring or "Parm" knife for the cheese, a butter knife to spread the cloves, and your baguette alongside.

For the perfect bite, tear off a piece of baguette, press a garlic clove or two out of its skin, and smear it on top. Hack off a nugget of Parm, place it on top, and drizzle with honey.

Tip When you're purchasing Parmigiano-Reggiano, make sure it's called exactly that (not just Parmesan) and has been aged for at least two years. The name, which will be stenciled into the rind, indicates a Denominazione di Origine Controllata (DOC) Parm that by law must be made in the northern Italian regions of Emilia-Romagna and Lombardy. The aging ensures fuller flavor. After you've used up the cheese, hang onto the rind (it'll keep indefinitely, tightly wrapped and frozen); it's a great flavor booster that can be added with the liquid when you're cooking soups, sauces (page 190), chilis, or stews. Remove and discard it after making the dish.

A Quick Cheese Platter Lesson

Rather than just serving a few hunks of cheese on a board, assemble a platter with know-how and creativity and make it memorable for your guests' eyes (and your Instagram feed; *see pages 50–51 for a photo*). In the winter, I love choosing different dried fruits and/or spreads to accompany each cheese. In the summer, use sliced fresh fruit and berries.

Blue Cheese

The sharpness of blues, from crumbly Stilton to creamy Danish to funky French Saint Agur, pairs nicely with sweet grapes, dates, and fresh or dried figs.

Chèvre (Goat Cheese)

I lean toward soft goat cheeses, which you might find fresh and rindless or soft-ripened with a thin, edible rind, such as Chabichon du Poitou or Crottin de Chavignol. I like to drizzle fresh logs with good-quality honey and ground or crushed pink peppercorns. When I buy the rind-on sorts, I enjoy them unadorned, accompanied by dried fruits (apricots pair well), nuts, and/or crackers.

Sharp Cheddar

Vermont's Cabot Creamery makes my favorite clothbound cheddar—it's aged in cloth as opposed to wax, resulting in a drier cheese with a deeper, richer flavor. It's fantastic with sweet spreads like pistachio butter or tart cherry or apricot preserves, and with Medjool dates. Cheddar is also great with savory pairings like cornichons and your favorite grainy mustard.

Emmental and Gruyère

These full-flavored, sweet but sharp, nutty mountain cheeses pair well with salted and roasted almonds, particularly Marcona, and cashews. Authentic Emmental (aka Emmentaler; Emmenthal) comes from Switzerland, but you'll also find excellent versions from France (Emmental de Savoie and raw-milk Emmental Grand Cru, for example) and Germany. The best Gruyère cheeses come from Switzerland and Germany, as well as France, where Beaufort, Emmental, and Comté (aka Gruyère de Comté) are made.

Stinky Cheeses

From creamy, sweet Robiola Piemonte to funky Epoisse and everything in between, these are best with hunks of fresh baguette. Stinky cheeses vary in texture and intensity, and are made with a variety of milks. Get to know them by trying different sorts.

Calculate 2 to 3 ounces of cheese per person. Select at least two or three cheeses, even for a small board, and let them come to room temperature before serving. Think about texture, flavor, milk type, style, and level of funkiness; it's nice to mix things up. You can create a theme (all cow's-milk cheeses or Spanish cheeses, for example), if you like, or keep it super simple. There are many ways to go and no hard-and-fast rules.

A Quick Cheese Platter Lesson
(page 49)

Cheesy Lemon-Rosemary Artichoke Dip

Makes 4 cups; serves 8

Decadent, flavorful, and perfect for anything from kettle chips or baguette to spears of endive (or your finger), this simple dip is a great gateway drug to a food coma. Using high-quality cheeses will make it memorable for your guests (or you alone on your couch—no judgment).

---

3 (6½-ounce) jars marinated artichokes, drained, coarsely chopped or quartered if whole

1 (8-ounce) package cream cheese, softened

6 ounces Gruyère, grated (1½ cups)

4 ounces aged sharp white cheddar (such as Cabot clothbound), grated (1 cup)

1 cup (8 ounces) full-fat sour cream

2 tablespoons fresh lemon juice

2 teaspoons finely chopped fresh rosemary

¼ teaspoon freshly ground black pepper

Toasted baguette slices, crudités, and/or your favorite crackers or chips for serving

Tip For the best taste and texture, go for artichokes marinated in oil (over the water-packed canned ones), in a jar or from the supermarket salad bar.

Heat the oven to 400°F, with a rack in the middle.

Combine all the dip ingredients in a large bowl and stir until smooth. Transfer to an 8-inch square baking dish, a 7- to 8-inch ovenproof skillet, or a 2-quart gratin dish.

Bake until the dip is bubbly and light golden brown on top, 22 to 25 minutes. Let cool for 7 to 10 minutes before serving. (I've burned my mouth more times than I care to admit.) Serve with toasted baguette slices, crudités, and/or crackers or chips.

Radishes in Pink Peppercorn-and-Chive Butter

Serves 4 to 6

One of my favorite restaurants, the NoMad in New York City, first brought this treat to my mouth's attention. It's both a savory play on white-chocolate-covered strawberries and a take on the French tradition of serving crisp radishes with butter and salt. In this case, the butter is partly melted and then whisked to make it glossy but still soft enough to evenly coat the radishes. It's seasoned with crushed pink peppercorns and chives. The radishes are given a quick dip and then a little chill in the fridge, which hardens the butter into a sheen.

2 bunches small to medium radishes (any variety)

8 tablespoons (1 stick) good-quality unsalted French, Irish, or Vermont butter (such as Kerrygold, Vermont Creamery, or your local favorite)

1 tablespoon finely chopped fresh chives

1 teaspoon pink peppercorns, crushed with your fingers

Flaky sea salt, such as Maldon

Line a baking sheet with parchment or wax paper. Rinse the radishes well, removing any dirt from the greens (especially at the base), then pat thoroughly dry. Trim the stems to ½ inch, leaving 1 or 2 small leaves, if you wish.

In a medium microwave-safe bowl, heat the butter for 10-second intervals, watching it carefully, until it is half melted, 30 to 40 seconds; the key is to have about half the stick of butter still intact.

Vigorously whisk the butter until it is completely opaque—it should be in a liquid state but the same color as a chilled stick. If it's translucent, you've overheated it. (Not to worry, just chill until solidified, then gently heat and whisk it again.) Fold in the chives, peppercorns, and ½ teaspoon flaky salt.

Pat the radishes dry again if they're at all damp. Dip one radish in the butter to coat, leaving a bit of the top exposed, and place on the prepared baking sheet. (If the coating is too thin or not sticking, wait 2 to 3 minutes for the butter to cool a bit and try again. If the butter becomes gloppy while you're dipping, it's cooled a bit too much; gently rewarm and whisk it again.) Repeat with the remaining radishes, then refrigerate the radishes until the butter is set, about 10 minutes. (*The radishes can be kept refrigerated, uncovered, for up to 8 hours.*) Serve the radishes on a wooden board or large platter with a mound of flaky salt alongside for dipping.

Tips If the only high-quality butter available is salted or lightly salted ("demi-sel"), leave out the crushed salt when you stir in the peppercorns and chives. If you don't have a microwave, melt the butter in a small saucepan over very low heat, occasionally lifting the pan off the heat and swirling, until the butter is just half melted.

Jonny's Queso Blanco

Makes about 3 cups; serves 4 to 6

My *Queer Eye* castmate and bestie Jonathan Van Ness would probably threaten my life if I did not include at least one recipe just for him, so I present you with his queso. While we were filming in Georgia, we would order bowls of this delectably gooey appetizer (or main, if you're us) at our go-to Tex-Mex restaurant in Atlanta. As Jonny pointed out—and continues to, wherever our travels take us—a good queso should be runny and—most important—there shouldn't be a leaf of cilantro in sight. While I wouldn't dare garnish this version of the dish with one of my favorite herbs, I couldn't help but add some crispy crumbled chorizo, which makes it (almost) a complete meal—right?

Tips

Be sure to purchase fresh chorizo (i.e., the Mexican-type version) for this recipe, not the dry cured and/or smoked Spanish type. It's found in many supermarkets—Wellshire Farms makes one—as well as in Latin and gourmet markets.

Ask for American cheese at the supermarket deli, where it's sold in bulk.

1 pound white American cheese (such as Land O'Lakes), coarsely chopped

1 cup whole milk

2 tablespoons unsalted butter

½ teaspoon ground cumin

¼ teaspoon garlic powder

1 (4.5-ounce) can chopped green chiles, drained

6 ounces fresh chorizo sausage, casings removed (see Tip)

Tortilla chips for serving

In a large heatproof bowl, combine the cheese, milk, butter, cumin, and garlic powder.

Fill a medium saucepan with 2 inches of water. Bring the water to a gentle simmer. Place the bowl with the cheese mixture on top of the pan and cook, stirring frequently, until the mixture is melted, smooth, and gently bubbling, 5 to 7 minutes. Stir in the chiles and remove from the heat.

Meanwhile, cook the chorizo in a medium skillet over medium-high heat, stirring occasionally with a wooden spoon and breaking up the sausage into small pieces, until the fat is rendered and the chorizo is really crispy, about 4 minutes. Remove from the heat.

Transfer the queso to a serving bowl. Using a slotted spoon, scoop the chorizo from the skillet and sprinkle it over the queso. Serve the queso hot, with tortilla chips for dipping.

Herbed Lobster and Saffron Dip

Makes 5½ cups; serves 8 to 10

This dip is an homage to one of my favorite French products, Boursin, a creamy, tangy, herbaceous French cheese that was the epitome of gourmet in North America in the 1970s and still deserves a place at the table. Folding in saffron and chunks of meaty lobster turns my version of the cheese into a chic party dish. Couple any leftovers (if you're lucky to have them) with good-quality shredded cheddar to make a very special grilled cheese sandwich.

¼ teaspoon packed crumbled saffron threads

2 (8-ounce) packages cream cheese, softened

½ cup mayonnaise

1 tablespoon grated lemon zest

2 tablespoons fresh lemon juice

2 garlic cloves, grated or minced

1 teaspoon kosher salt, or to taste

¼ teaspoon freshly ground black pepper, or to taste

1 pound cooked lobster meat (see Tip), cut into 1-inch chunks (about 2¾ cups)

6 ounces Parmesan, preferably Parmigiano-Reggiano, finely grated (1½ cups)

3 tablespoons finely chopped fresh basil

1 tablespoon finely chopped fresh dill

1 tablespoon finely chopped fresh chives

Assorted crudités (such as carrots, celery, bell pepper, snap peas, radishes, cherry tomatoes, and endive), waffle potato chips, and/or Ritz crackers for serving

In a small bowl, combine the saffron and 2 tablespoons hot water. Let stand until the water has turned a deep orange, about 10 minutes.

Meanwhile, combine the cream cheese, mayonnaise, lemon zest, lemon juice, garlic, salt, and pepper in a large bowl and beat with an electric mixer on medium-high until airy and smooth, 1 to 2 minutes.

Fold the saffron mixture into the cream cheese mixture to combine, then fold in the lobster, Parmesan, and herbs. Adjust the seasoning to taste.

Transfer the dip to a serving dish and chill for at least 30 minutes, or up to 6 hours, to allow the flavors to blend. Let stand at room temperature for 15 to 30 minutes before serving.

Serve the dip with your choice of crudités, chips, and/or Ritz crackers.

Tip

You can purchase cooked lobster meat for this recipe, or cook 3 (1½-pound) lobsters to get 1 pound cooked meat.

Olive Oil and Pepper–Marinated Watermelon Bites with Halloumi

Serves 6 to 8

This dish is one of my go-tos for summer entertaining: bites of sweet watermelon marinated in good-quality olive oil and coarsely cracked peppercorns, topped with salty grilled halloumi cheese and fresh mint. Refreshing, beautiful, and super easy to prepare.

---

32 (1-inch) cubes seedless watermelon (from a 4-pound melon)

¼ cup extra-virgin olive oil

1 tablespoon freshly ground black pepper or mixed peppercorns

1 (8- to 9-ounce) package halloumi cheese, drained and cut lengthwise into 4 slices

A good-sized handful of fresh mint leaves, large leaves roughly torn

In a bowl, combine the watermelon, oil, and pepper. Let stand for 10 to 15 minutes, gently stirring occasionally.

Pat the halloumi slices dry with paper towels. Heat a large dry nonstick skillet over medium-high heat. Add the halloumi and cook, turning once, until golden brown on both sides, 4 to 6 minutes. Transfer the cheese slices to a cutting board and cut each one into 8 pieces.

Reserving the oil, use a slotted spoon to transfer the watermelon to a large serving platter. Set a piece of halloumi on each watermelon cube, then top with a mint leaf. Drizzle the bites with about 3 tablespoons of the reserved oil, spooning a healthy dose of the cracked peppercorns on top as you go. Serve immediately (it's tastiest while the cheese is warm), inviting your guests to eat with their fingers.

Tip Halloumi is a semi-hard brined cheese, traditionally from Cyprus, that holds up very well to heat (it is often grilled). Look for it in well-stocked supermarkets or at cheese shops. If you can't find it, use squares of your favorite feta instead and don't cook it. If the pieces of cheese aren't perfectly cut, no stress—irregular-shaped chunks are totally fine.

Ricotta

with Pickled Wild Mushrooms, Toasted Hazelnuts + Honey

Serves 4 to 6

When I was a kid, my parents would take me mushroom picking in the Eastern Townships in Canada. Morels were the prize for my mother, but my favorites were sweet chanterelles and meaty boletes (cèpes). Pickling these beauties ensured we could enjoy them in the following months and at Christmas and Easter, as part of our Polish dinner or brunch spreads. In addition to high-quality pickled mushrooms (which you can make or purchase), good/fresh ricotta is key here. If you don't have an old-school Italian grocery or farmers' market (where the very best fresh ricotta generally comes from), just please buy the full-fat variety, which will be richer in flavor and more deeply milky than its reduced-fat counterpart.

The brand Vavel makes delicious pickled mushrooms. Find them at Polish markets and online.

⅓ cup hazelnuts

1 (15-ounce) container whole-milk ricotta

2 tablespoons honey

Freshly ground black pepper

½ cup drained pickled chanterelles or other wild mushrooms, store-bought or homemade (page 64), halved or quartered if large

About 2 tablespoons extra-virgin olive oil

Flaky sea salt, such as Maldon

¼ cup loosely packed celery leaves (from the heart of the bunch), large leaves torn

Celery sticks for serving

Crackers for serving (optional)

Heat the oven to 350°F, with a rack in the middle.

Spread the hazelnuts on a baking sheet and toast in the oven until fragrant and lightly golden, with blistered skins, 7 to 12 minutes. Remove from the oven and wrap the nuts in a clean kitchen towel. Let steam for 1 minute, then rub the nuts in the towel to remove the skins (it's fine if not all the skins come off). Let cool completely, about 10 minutes, then coarsely chop.

Spread the ricotta into a nice thin round on a large serving plate. Drizzle with the honey, then season generously with pepper. Sprinkle the chopped hazelnuts evenly over the top, and then the mushrooms. Drizzle with 2 tablespoons oil and sprinkle with a generous pinch or two of flaky salt.

In a small bowl, toss together the celery leaves with ¼ teaspoon oil and a pinch of flaky salt. Sprinkle over the ricotta.

Serve with celery sticks and crackers, if desired.

Continues

Pickled Wild Mushrooms

Makes 1 cup

Pickled mushrooms are great with the ricotta on page 63, and terrific as part of a cheese board (page 49), atop rye toast with butter, in bitter green salads, or as a pizza topping.

1 cup white wine vinegar

1 tablespoon sugar

3 garlic cloves, gently smashed and peeled

1 sprig fresh rosemary

¼ teaspoon kosher salt

About 5 ounces wild mushrooms, stem ends trimmed, halved or quartered if large

In a medium saucepan, bring the vinegar, sugar, garlic, rosemary, and salt just to a boil, stirring occasionally to dissolve the sugar. Remove the pan from the heat and stir in the mushrooms. Cover the pan and let stand until the mushrooms are flavorful, 10 to 15 minutes.

If serving immediately, drain and serve. Or let cool completely in the brine, then transfer the mushrooms and brine to a jar, cover, and refrigerate for up to 1 week.

Spicy Fennel Frico

Makes about 4½ dozen; serves 8 to 10

I first tried a version of these snacks at Marc Vetri's restaurant Cucina Vetri in Philadelphia and was struck by how simple yet perfect they were. Thinly sliced and lightly caramelized around the edges, with some melty cheese on top and a little red pepper kick, the vegetable becomes an elegant treat. I call these frico because they recall those lacy baked Parmesan cheese rounds, though they aren't as crisp. Serve them with cocktails.

1 large fennel bulb (about 1 pound without stalks), trimmed, leaving the root end intact

2¼ cups grated Parmigiano-Reggiano or Grana Padano (about 8 ounces)

Kosher salt

¾ teaspoon red pepper flakes

1 to 2 large lemons

The cheese melts and sets best in this recipe when it is grated on a Microplane or the small holes of a box grater.

Heat the oven to 400°F, with racks in the middle and upper thirds. Line two baking sheets with parchment paper.

Using a sharp chef's knife, cut the fennel bulb lengthwise in half. Place one half flat side down on your cutting board and slice it lengthwise into very thin slices, $\frac{1}{16}$ to ⅛ inch thick (the thinner the better; any end pieces that fall apart can be pushed back together in the shape of a slice or saved for another use). Repeat with the remaining half bulb.

Spread 1 teaspoon of the Parmesan on one of the baking sheets to just about the size of a fennel slice. Top with a fennel slice. Repeat, spacing the cheese and fennel slices about ½ inch apart, until your baking sheets are filled. (You'll use about half of the total slices and half the cheese.)

Sprinkle a tiny pinch of salt over each fennel slice, then thinly cover each with 1 teaspoon more cheese. Sprinkle the slices with about half the red pepper flakes, then grate a little lemon zest over the top.

Bake, rotating the sheets and switching their positions halfway through, until the cheese is bubbling and golden, 8 to 10 minutes.

Slide the parchment onto wire racks and let the frico cool, 4 to 5 minutes (the cheese will set and crisp a bit). Repeat, cooling and relining the baking sheets. Serve warm or at room temperature.

Hi-Lo Poutine

Serves 4 to 6 as a side dish or snack

Poutine—that Québécois favorite of French fries topped with melty cheese curds and gravy—is a classic in Montreal, where I grew up. It's the favored post-night-out vodka-absorber at late-night eateries and diners. In recent years, though, famous Québécois chefs—Chuck Hughes and Martin Picard among them—have elevated the dish, adding luxe ingredients like butter-poached lobster and foie gras. My take on the marriage of high and low involves pairing America's beloved Tater Tots with a green-peppercorn demi-glace that replaces the traditional gravy and takes merely minutes to make.

Tips

Demi-glace is a reduced rich meat stock. For this recipe, buy a demi-glace concentrate such as More Than Gourmet Glace de Veau Gold. You'll find it in large supermarkets, near the broths and/or spices, and online.

Cheese curds, tangy chunks of mild, fresh cheese that are delicious eaten out of hand as a snack and great for melting, are found in cheese shops, larger supermarkets, and online. They're sometimes called "squeaky cheese," for the sound they make when you bite into them.

1 (28-ounce) bag frozen Tater Tots, preferably "Extra Crispy"

1 (1.5-ounce) container beef or veal demi-glace, dissolved in water to make 1 cup (follow the package instructions)

2½ teaspoons apple cider vinegar

1 bay leaf

1 tablespoon unsalted butter, chilled

1 teaspoon green peppercorns, coarsely chopped

¼ teaspoon kosher salt

6 ounces (about 1¼ cups) cheese curds (see Tip), broken into small nuggets, at room temperature

1 tablespoon finely chopped fresh chives

Bake the Tater Tots as instructed on the package (leave some space between them on your baking sheet to help facilitate browning).

Meanwhile, in a small saucepan, bring the demi-glace mixture, vinegar, and bay leaf to a simmer over medium-high heat and simmer until the sauce is slightly thickened, 2 to 3 minutes. Remove from the heat and whisk in the cold butter until the butter is just melted and the sauce is smooth. Stir in the green peppercorns and salt. Remove and discard the bay leaf.

Place half of the piping-hot Tater Tots in a large shallow bowl. Sprinkle with half of the cheese curds and chives, then drizzle half of the sauce on top. Repeat to make a second layer. Serve immediately.

Alsatian Tart Three Ways

An Alsatian tart (also known as *tarte flambée*) is more like a flatbread than a tart. Here are three of my favorite versions. The no-fuss crust is made with store-bought pizza dough, which you can top with whatever you like. A good rule of thumb when making up your own combinations is to keep it fairly simple and on the lighter side, weight-wise. Going with just three to four ingredients allows each one to shine, and it keeps the toppings from toppling off the crust as you're eating. *The photo is on pages 70–71.*

Alsatian Tart with Charred Red Onions and Crème Fraîche

Makes twelve 4-inch squares

This rustic yet chic tart is a great vegetarian option. It makes me think of French onion soup in tart form, which isn't the worst thing in the world.

Olive oil for the griddle/grill pan

4 medium red onions (about 2 pounds), cut into ½-inch-thick wedges, leaving some of the root end intact

Alsatian Tart Crust (at right), warm

1 cup (8 ounces) crème fraîche, well stirred

Extra-virgin olive oil for drizzling

Flaky sea salt, such as Maldon

Freshly ground black pepper

Chopped fennel fronds or chives for sprinkling (optional)

Heat a griddle or grill pan over medium-high heat. Brush lightly with oil. Arrange the onion wedges on the hot pan, cut side down, and grill, without disturbing, until the bottom sides are deeply golden and charred in spots, 5 to 6 minutes. Turn the wedges over and grill until the second sides are golden and the onions are crisp-tender, 5 to 6 minutes more. Transfer to a plate.

Place the warm crust on a large cutting board (cool if it's still hot) and spread the crème fraîche over it, leaving about a ¼-inch border. Arrange the charred onions on top. Cut the tart into 12 pieces and lightly drizzle with olive oil. Sprinkle with flaky salt, pepper, and fennel fronds or chives, if using, and serve.

ALSATIAN TART CRUST

Makes 1 crust

Pizza dough can be purchased from well-stocked grocery stores or your local pizza shop. Give the dough time to come to room temperature before using, which will allow it to stretch.

2 tablespoons cornmeal, plus more if needed

1 tablespoon extra-virgin olive oil

1 pound store-bought white or whole wheat pizza dough, at room temperature

Heat the oven to 425°F, with a rack in the middle.

Dust a 13-x-18-inch baking sheet with 1 tablespoon of the cornmeal, then drizzle with the oil. Place the dough on the baking sheet and gently press and stretch it out to the pan edges, dusting your hands and/or the dough with a little cornmeal if the dough is too sticky. (If the dough springs back, let it rest for a few minutes, then resume; it'll get there!) Dust the top of the dough with the remaining tablespoon of cornmeal, then prick all over with the tines of a fork.

Bake until the bottom of the crust and the edges are golden, 14 to 16 minutes. Transfer to a wire rack and let cool. The crust can be baked up to 8 hours ahead and kept uncovered at room temperature. Rewarm in a 225°F oven for a few minutes, if necessary, before topping.

continues

Alsatian Tart Three Ways
(pages 69–73)

Alsatian Tart with Melted Leeks, Gruyère, and Prosciutto

Makes twelve 4-inch squares

This trio of toppings recalls the much-loved French combination of leeks, cheese, and bacon. Also, I love saying "melted leeks." Say it and try not to smile.

6 medium leeks (2¼ to 2½ pounds)

2 tablespoons unsalted butter

2 tablespoons extra-virgin olive oil

½ teaspoon kosher salt

5 ounces thinly sliced prosciutto, preferably the packaged sort (from 2 packages)

Alsatian Tart Crust (page 69), warm or cooled

3 ounces Gruyère or Emmenthaler, coarsely grated (about 1 heaping cup)

Fresh thyme leaves for sprinkling

Heat the oven to 350°F, with racks in the middle and upper third. Line two baking sheets with parchment paper.

Trim off and discard the root ends and tough green tops of the leeks. Cut the remaining parts lengthwise in half, then cut into 1-inch pieces. Submerge in a large bowl of cold water and swish the leeks around, separating the layers to remove the grit. Lift the leeks out of the water and transfer to a colander to drain. Spin-dry in a salad spinner or pat dry with a dishcloth.

In large skillet or Dutch oven, heat the butter and oil over medium heat until the butter is melted. Add the leeks and cook, stirring occasionally and reducing the heat if the leeks begin to brown, until softened, 25 to 30 minutes. Add the salt and continue cooking, stirring occasionally, until the leeks are very soft and "melted," 10 to 15 minutes more. Remove from the heat.

Meanwhile, arrange the prosciutto slices on the baking sheets, leaving a little space between them. Bake until the slices are shriveled and dark red and the fatty edges are golden, 12 to 15 minutes; keep an eye on them to avoid burning. Place the prosciutto "chips" on a wire rack set over a baking sheet; they will crisp as they cool.

Break the prosciutto chips into 1- to 2-inch pieces and set aside. Heat the oven to broil, with the rack 4 to 5 inches from the heat source.

Spread the leeks on top of the baked crust. Sprinkle with the cheese. Broil the tart until the top is bubbling and golden, 2 to 3 minutes. Transfer to a large cutting board. Cut into 12 pieces, top with the prosciutto chips and thyme, and serve.

Packaged sliced prosciutto is the perfect thickness for crisping in the oven. And since the slices come separated by nice neat sheets of paper, it's quick and easy to get them from the package to the pan without tearing.

Alsatian Tart with Miso-Glazed Squash

Makes twelve 4-inch squares

During my days as a waiter and manager at Bond Street restaurant in New York City, I was introduced to the technique of using miso in a glaze on everything from winter squash to fish. Kabocha squash has a sweeter flesh and drier texture than many other varieties, and it's worth looking for at farmers' markets.

1 large winter squash (2¼ to 2½ pounds), preferably Kabocha, Red Kuri, or butternut

3 tablespoons extra-virgin olive oil

½ teaspoon kosher salt

3 tablespoons dry fruity white wine, such as Viognier or unoaked Chardonnay

2 tablespoons mirin

2 tablespoons sugar

1 tablespoon white miso

Freshly ground black pepper

Alsatian Tart Crust (page 69), warm or cooled

2 tablespoons hot pepper sesame oil or toasted sesame oil plus red pepper flakes to taste

1 heaping teaspoon furikake (see Tip) or toasted black or white sesame seeds

3 tablespoons coarsely chopped fresh cilantro

Heat the oven to 450°F, with racks in the middle and upper thirds. Line two baking sheets with parchment paper.

Cut the squash in half (no need to peel if you are using the suggested varieties), then remove the seeds. Place each half cut side down on a cutting board and cut lengthwise into ⅓-inch-thick slices.

Divide the squash slices between the baking sheets. Drizzle with the oil and sprinkle with the salt. Toss gently to coat, then arrange cut side down on the pans. Roast, rotating the pans once halfway through, until the squash is crisp-tender, about 10 minutes.

Meanwhile, combine the wine, mirin, and sugar in a small saucepan and bring just to a boil over medium heat, whisking frequently to dissolve the sugar. Reduce to a simmer, then whisk in the miso and continue simmering, whisking occasionally, until the glaze is thickened, syrupy, and reduced to about a generous ¼ cup, 4 to 6 minutes more. Remove from the heat.

When the squash is ready, brush with the miso glaze. Return to the oven and continue roasting until the squash is tender and the glaze is bubbling, 4 to 6 minutes. Remove from the oven and sprinkle with pepper. Let cool for 5 to 10 minutes.

Transfer the baked crust to a large cutting board. Drizzle the hot sesame oil over the top. (Or, if you are using toasted sesame oil, drizzle over the crust, then sprinkle with red pepper flakes to taste.) Arrange the squash on top (overlapping the pieces a little if necessary). Sprinkle with the furikake or sesame seeds and cilantro. Cut into 12 pieces and serve.

Furikake is a Japanese rice seasoning typically made of dried fish flakes, sesame seeds, and dried nori, although it may also include other seasonings. I sprinkle it over salads, vegetables, and fish. Look for it in the ethnic or spice sections of larger supermarkets, or buy it online.

GREENS, VEG, AND OTHER SIDES

Serves 4 to 6

Grilled Kale Caesar

On family trips to Ottawa, my Uncle Andy and his family always greeted us with a steakhouse-worthy spread. My favorite dish was his Caesar salad with wedges of romaine and a tangy, salty, spicy dressing. I've updated it by charring whole lacinato kale leaves on the grill and serving them on a big platter, drizzled with my own version of Uncle Andy's family-famous sauce. A generous dose of cracked black pepper gives the dish an extra kick. Lacinato kale has long, crinkled dark-green leaves that crisp up nicely in spots when grilled.

Tip Sacrilegious as it may seem to cheese snobs, the pre-grated Parm you find in the refrigerated section of the supermarket (*not* the infamous green can) offers a nice grittiness here. If you're going with real Parmigiano-Reggiano, you can get a similar effect by grating the cheese on the small star-shaped holes of a box grater.

DRESSING

1 garlic clove, thinly sliced

3/4 teaspoon kosher salt

4 anchovy fillets, coarsely chopped

1/2 cup finely grated Parmesan, preferably pre-grated (see Tip), or Parmigiano-Reggiano (about 2 ounces)

2 large egg yolks

1 packed teaspoon finely grated lemon zest

3 tablespoons fresh lemon juice

2 teaspoons Dijon mustard

1 teaspoon honey

1 teaspoon Worcestershire sauce

3 to 5 dashes hot sauce, such as Tabasco

1/2 cup extra-virgin olive oil

Freshly ground black pepper

SALAD

2 bunches lacinato kale (about 1 pound), thick fibrous ends trimmed, leaves left whole, rinsed, and patted dry

Kosher salt

Extra-virgin olive oil

For the dressing: Mound the garlic and salt on a cutting board. Using a chef's knife, mash and chop into a paste. On the same board, finely chop the anchovy fillets, then chop and smear them into the garlic paste.

In a medium bowl, whisk together the garlic paste, Parm, egg yolks, lemon zest and juice, Dijon, honey, Worcestershire, hot sauce, oil, and a generous pinch or two of pepper. Taste the dressing and make sure it's salty enough and well balanced. There should be a nice kick from the hot sauce, acidity from the lemon, and a tiny hint of sweetness from the honey to round it all out. Adjust the seasoning to taste.

For the salad: Heat a gas or charcoal grill to medium-high or heat a grill pan over medium-high heat. (On a charcoal grill, most of the coals should be covered with white ash, and you should be able to hold your palm an inch or two above the cooking grate for no more than 2 to 3 seconds.)

In a large bowl, toss the kale with a generous pinch of salt and just enough oil to lightly coat. Grill the leaves, in batches if necessary, turning once, until you get a nice char, about 2 minutes per side.

Arrange the grilled leaves on a large serving platter, drizzling each one with dressing as you go and layering the leaves if necessary. Serve with knives and forks, or, better yet, eat with your fingers.

Roman Frisée and Sugar Snap Salad

Serves 4

One of my best discoveries in Rome was a salad, available only during the winter months, that was made with puntarelle, a variety of chicory. The nonna at the restaurant soaked the sliced greens in ice water to lessen the bitterness and give them a lovely curl. Since puntarella is hard to come by in the U.S., I make my version with frisée, and, because I love peas, I add sugar snaps. Slicing the peas allows the dressing to seep into the inner cavity of each. When they are not in season, it's better to leave them out. This simple salad is the essence of Italian cuisine, in which a few high-quality ingredients make for an incredible dish.

A small hunk of Pecorino Romano (about 4 ounces)

1 small garlic clove, thinly sliced

¼ teaspoon kosher salt

6 anchovy fillets, finely chopped

3 tablespoons extra-virgin olive oil

1 tablespoon fresh lemon juice

½ pound frisée, trimmed and separated into leaves

⅓ pound sugar snap peas, trimmed, strings removed, peas thinly sliced lengthwise

Freshly ground black pepper

Tip If you can't find frisée, try torn escarole or even romaine. The latter, while not a bitter green, has sturdy leaves that hold up well in this salad.

Finely grate enough of the cheese to yield ⅓ cup. Set aside.

Mound the garlic and salt on a cutting board. Using a chef's knife, mash and chop together to form a paste. On the same board, finely chop the anchovy fillets, then chop and smear them into the paste.

Transfer the garlic paste to a large bowl. Add the grated cheese and stir to combine, then whisk in the oil and lemon juice. Add the frisée and snap peas and toss to coat with the dressing.

Mound the salad on serving plates. Season with pepper to taste. Using a vegetable peeler or cheese plane, shave more cheese over the top.

Grilled Peach + Tomato Salad

WITH CRUNCHY ALMONDS

Serves 4

A perfect peach is just poetry. In this salad, the fruit's sweetness mingles with the bright, tangy juices of tomatoes, savory herbs, fruity olive oil, and a light touch of cheese. Heaven. This dish is a great accompaniment to a big grilled steak or vegetarian summer meal. I've made it with yellow or white peaches, donut peaches, and even nectarines, and all sorts of tomatoes (opt for heirlooms whenever you can). Pick whatever looks ripest and best at the market that day, and choose peaches and tomatoes that are relatively similar in size for the prettiest presentation.

Tip The peaches should be firm but ripe. Grilling them releases their juices, but they should have a bit of juice in them at the outset to get the ball rolling.

1 tablespoon extra-virgin olive oil, plus more for the grill

3 medium firm-ripe yellow or white peaches (about 1¼ pounds), cut into ¾-inch-thick wedges

¼ cup loosely packed fresh basil leaves

2 medium tomatoes (any color or variety; about 1 pound), cut into ¾-inch-thick wedges

Flaky sea salt, such as Maldon

1 teaspoon champagne vinegar or white wine vinegar

2- to 3-ounce hunk of Parmigiano-Reggiano

¼ cup roasted salted almonds, preferably Marcona, coarsely chopped

Heat a gas or charcoal grill to medium-high or heat a grill pan over medium-high heat. (On a charcoal grill, most of the coals should be covered with white ash, and you should be able to hold your palm an inch or two above the cooking grate for no more than 2 to 3 seconds.) Lightly oil the grill grate.

Grill the peaches cut side down until nicely charred, 1 to 2 minutes, then turn and grill until lightly charred on the second cut side, another 1 minute or so. Transfer to a plate and let cool to room temperature.

Meanwhile, stack the basil leaves on top of each other, tightly roll up lengthwise, and slice crosswise into thin ribbons.

Arrange the peach and tomato wedges on a serving platter, alternating them in any sort of pattern you like (circles or rows). Top with several pinches of flaky salt, then drizzle with the oil and vinegar. Shave the cheese over the top, then sprinkle with the basil and almonds.

Southern Italian/ Cold NYC Winter Salad

Serves 4

In the winter, when I long for fresh produce, I serve this citrus and fennel salad, which reminds me of Italy. Cutting the fennel as thin as humanly possible dials back some of the intensity of the anisey flavor, giving you more delicate but still crunchy strands of translucent goodness. Chilling the citrus makes the salad extra refreshing.

Tip I like to use a mix of citrus here, because I love the variety of flavors—some sweet, others tangy. (Plus, the colors!) But you can also go single citrus, if you want to—this recipe is flexible. Purchase whatever you like best.

2 tablespoons shelled unsalted pistachios

About 2 tablespoons extra-virgin olive oil

Kosher salt

2 blood oranges or Cara Cara oranges, chilled

1 pink grapefruit, preferably small, chilled

1 navel orange, chilled

1 medium to large fennel bulb, preferably with fronds, stalks removed and fronds reserved (optional); bulb cut lengthwise in half, cored, and very thinly sliced

Flaky sea salt, such as Maldon

Freshly ground black pepper

1½ tablespoons fresh lemon juice

Heat the oven to 350°F, with a rack in the middle.

Spread the pistachios on a small baking sheet (or use a pie pan) and toast until fragrant, 4 to 5 minutes. Remove from the oven and immediately toss with ½ teaspoon oil and a generous pinch of kosher salt, then transfer to a plate to cool. Coarsely chop.

Using a sharp paring knife, trim off the tops and bottoms of the citrus fruits to expose the flesh. Stand one piece of fruit on end and cut away the peel and white pith, following the curve of the fruit from top to bottom. Repeat with the remaining citrus, then cut all the fruit crosswise into ¼-inch-thick slices. Cut one slice (your choice of fruit) into small wedges and set aside for garnish. Arrange the remaining slices slightly overlapping on a serving platter.

In a medium bowl, toss together the fennel, a generous pinch each of flaky salt and pepper, and 2 tablespoons oil, then arrange over the citrus. If you have fennel fronds, coarsely chop enough to yield 1 to 2 tablespoons.

Drizzle the salad with the lemon juice, then top with the pistachios, reserved citrus pieces, a couple good pinches of flaky salt, and the fennel fronds, if using.

Duck Fat–Roasted Potato Salad with Mustardy Sauce

Serves 4 to 6

This decadent rustic salad was inspired by a recipe for duck fat–roasted potatoes, made by my dear friend and mentor Ted Allen. I serve it with a lemony yogurt for dipping or swooshing—depending on whether you're eating with your fingers or with a fork. Although the salad is good at room temp for summer dinners or picnics, it's fantastic warm alongside Crispy-Skin Salmon (page 174), Chile-Maple Roasted Chicken (page 216), or Rosemary Pork Tenderloin (page 228).

Duck fat is high in unsaturated and monounsaturated fats (the good kinds). It's sold at gourmet markets and online, and it keeps well refrigerated for up to 6 months, or frozen indefinitely. I like to freeze it in small portions in ice cube trays, then pop out the frozen cubes and keep them in the freezer in a resealable bag. This way I don't have to thaw and refreeze larger amounts. If you can't get duck fat, you can sub olive oil in this recipe.

POTATOES

2 pounds fingerling potatoes or other small potatoes, scrubbed and cut lengthwise in half

2 tablespoons duck fat, at room temperature (or substitute extra-virgin olive oil)

Kosher salt

6 ounces thick-sliced pancetta, cut into 1⁄4-inch cubes, or thick-cut bacon, cut crosswise into 1⁄2-inch-wide pieces

3 tablespoons coarsely chopped fresh tarragon

Freshly ground black pepper

DRESSING

1⁄4 cup extra-virgin olive oil

1 tablespoon red wine vinegar

2 teaspoons grainy Dijon mustard

1 3⁄4 teaspoons fresh lemon juice

1 1⁄2 teaspoons honey

1⁄4 teaspoon kosher salt

1⁄4 teaspoon coarsely ground black pepper

YOGURT

1 1⁄2 cups whole-milk Greek yogurt

2 teaspoons grated lemon zest

1 1⁄4 teaspoons fresh lemon juice

1⁄4 teaspoon kosher salt

1⁄8 teaspoon freshly ground black pepper

For the potatoes: Heat the oven to 425°F, with a rack in the middle.

Put the potatoes on a baking sheet and toss together with the duck fat (or oil) and ½ teaspoon salt. Arrange the potatoes cut side down on the sheet, leaving space between them to ensure a crisp brown finish, and roast until deeply golden, 25 to 30 minutes.

Meanwhile, place the pancetta or bacon in a large skillet and cook over medium-high heat, stirring occasionally, until golden and crispy all over, 8 to 12 minutes. Using a slotted spoon, transfer to paper towels to drain.

For the dressing: In a large bowl, whisk together all the ingredients until well combined.

For the yogurt: In a bowl, stir together all the ingredients.

When your crispy potato babies are ready, transfer them to the bowl with the dressing. Add the pancetta and tarragon and toss to combine. Season with salt and pepper to taste.

Serve hot, warm, or at room temperature, with the yogurt on the side or dolloped on top.

Carrot Ribbon Salad

with Ginger, Parsley + Dates

Serves 4

This salad evolved from my father's favorite road-trip snack—carrot sticks with roasted almonds, lemon juice, and salt. I've punched it up with fresh ginger, lots of parsley, and dates (you can almost feel the antioxidants at work!). I peel the carrots into thin ribbons so they crisp up and curl after a short soak in ice water. For even more beauty, try different colors of carrots.

---

1 pound medium carrots (about 6), preferably rainbow

2 tablespoons extra-virgin olive oil

2 tablespoons fresh lemon juice

1 teaspoon grated peeled fresh ginger

3/4 teaspoon honey

Kosher salt

1/3 cup finely chopped fresh flat-leaf parsley

1/2 cup roasted salted almonds, coarsely chopped

6 large Medjool dates, pitted and thinly sliced lengthwise

Using a vegetable peeler, shave the carrots into long, thin slices, watching out for your fingers. Soak, along with any remaining carrot nubs, in a bowl of ice water until the slices curl, about 15 minutes. Drain and pat dry.

In a large salad bowl, whisk together the oil, lemon juice, ginger, honey, and 1/8 teaspoon salt. Add the carrots, parsley, half the almonds, and half the dates and toss to combine. Adjust the salt to taste.

Top the salad with the remaining almonds and dates and serve.

Tip I like Y-shaped peelers because of their super-sharp blades and easy-to-grip handles. To peel fresh ginger quickly and easily, use the tip of a small spoon to scrape away the skin.

Asparagus with Oozy Eggs

Serves 4 to 6

Eggs and asparagus are as iconic a pairing as the Queen and her corgis. In this version, the asparagus is roasted, then covered with mashed soft-cooked eggs with liquid-gold yolks and sprinkled with crispy bits of salty, meaty pancetta. A little bit of vinegar brightens up the dish, balancing the fat and turning the runny eggs into a dressing of sorts. Serve this with both forks *and* spoons.

1½ pounds asparagus, preferably medium

1½ tablespoons extra-virgin olive oil

1 teaspoon fresh thyme leaves

Kosher salt

4 large eggs

1 (¼-pound) chunk pancetta, cut into ⅓-inch cubes

1½ teaspoons red wine vinegar

Freshly ground black pepper

Heat the oven to 425°F, with a rack in the lower third.

Cut off and discard 1 inch from the bottom ends of the asparagus. Then, using a vegetable peeler, peel the lower 1 to 2 inches of the stalks. Put the asparagus on a baking sheet and toss with the oil, thyme, and ⅛ teaspoon salt. Spread out the asparagus and roast until the spears are tender but still have a good bite, 12 to 15 minutes.

Meanwhile, fill a medium saucepan with 3 inches of water and bring to a simmer. Using a slotted spoon, gently lower the eggs into the water, taking care not to drop them. Cook for exactly 6 minutes, then transfer the eggs to a bowl of ice water and let cool for about 5 minutes. Drain, gently peel, and place in a small bowl.

While the eggs are cooking, cook the pancetta in a dry skillet over medium heat, stirring occasionally, until the pieces are golden and most of their fat has rendered, 6 to 7 minutes. Remove from the heat and set aside.

Using a fork, mash the eggs with the vinegar and a scant ½ teaspoon salt until a slightly frothy sauce forms.

Arrange the asparagus on a serving platter. Drizzle with the oozy egg mixture, then top with the crispy pancetta and a generous pinch or two of pepper.

Tip Many cooks just snap off the ends of asparagus, which removes the tough, woody parts, but it also often takes off some of the edible portion. A less wasteful way to go is to cut off and discard about 1 inch from the bottom of each spear, then use a vegetable peeler to remove an inch or two of the peel from the freshly cut bottoms. This is especially important for thicker asparagus, since the peels get tougher as the stalks grow.

Crispy Brussels Sprouts with Prosciutto Chips

Serves 4

Brussels sprouts are one of my favorite vegetables, and I've had them every which way. At home, I always come back to keeping them simple: charred on the outside, with a nice firm-tender bite in the center. Prosciutto chips add a deliciously smoky, meaty umami bite.

---

3 ounces thinly sliced prosciutto, preferably the packaged sort

1½ pounds Brussels sprouts

3 tablespoons unsalted butter

3 tablespoons extra-virgin olive oil

Kosher salt

2 teaspoons finely grated lemon zest

2 tablespoons fresh lemon juice

Heat the oven to 350°F, with a rack in the middle. Line a baking sheet with parchment paper.

Arrange the prosciutto slices on the baking sheet, leaving a little space between them. Bake until they are shriveled and dark red and the fatty edges are golden, 12 to 15 minutes; keep an eye on them to prevent burning. Place the prosciutto "chips" on a wire rack set over a baking sheet to cool; they will crisp as they cool.

Cutting a little V into the base of each sprout makes for even cooking while keeping the leaves intact.

Meanwhile, cut the Brussels sprouts lengthwise in half through the stem end. Make a V-shaped incision at the base of each sprout half. Remove and discard any blemished outer leaves.

Heat 1 tablespoon of the butter and 1 tablespoon of the oil in a large skillet, preferably cast-iron, over medium-high heat until the foam subsides. (The pan needs to be superhot, so test it with a sprout leaf to see if it crisps upon contact.) Place about one third of the Brussels sprouts in the pan, arranging them so they are mostly cut side down, with a little space between them. Reduce the heat to medium and cook until the undersides are deeply golden, about 3 minutes. Turn the sprouts over, sprinkle with a pinch of salt, and continue cooking until golden and tender, 3 to 4 minutes more. Using a slotted spoon, transfer the Brussels sprouts to a large serving bowl. Repeat with the remaining butter, oil, and sprouts.

Crumble the prosciutto chips into small pieces and add to the bowl with the Brussels sprouts. Add the lemon zest and lemon juice, then toss to combine. Season with salt to taste. Serve hot.

Braised Red Cabbage with Pears + Cumin

Serves 4 to 6

The Polish boy in me longs for this classic on cold winter nights. Braising is a simple technique that concentrates flavors by using low heat, a bit of liquid, and a sealed or partially covered pot. Pears offer a nice change of pace from the usual apple in this dish, and I love the way their sweet gritty texture half dissolves and cooks into the vinegar and cabbage juices. A knob of butter stirred in at the end adds a glossy sheen and the perfect little touch of fat (read: flavor boost), but you can leave it out, if you prefer. This makes a great side for Pork Chop like at Kiki's Taverna (page 225) or Kielbasa Polish-Style (page 199). But I often pair it with a bunch of sides for a meat-free spread. *The photograph is on page 227.*

---

2 firm-ripe Bosc or Bartlett pears

3 tablespoons olive oil

1 large red cabbage (2 to 2½ pounds), quartered, cored, and cut crosswise into thin strips

2 bay leaves

½ teaspoon cumin seeds

Kosher salt

¼ cup plus 2 tablespoons apple cider vinegar

2 tablespoons honey

1 tablespoon unsalted butter (optional)

Freshly ground black pepper

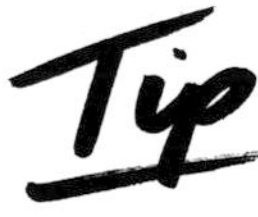

Like any braised dish, this tastes even better a day or two after you make it. To warm it before serving, gently heat it in a covered pot over low heat, with 1 to 2 tablespoons of water added.

Quarter and core the pears. Coarsely grate them or cut them into ¼-inch pieces.

Heat the oil in a large Dutch oven or other wide heavy pot with a lid over medium heat. Add the pears, then stir in the cabbage, bay leaves, cumin seeds, and ½ teaspoon salt and cook, stirring frequently, until the cabbage begins to wilt, about 5 minutes.

Add ¼ cup of the vinegar and 2 tablespoons water. Cover the pot and gently simmer over medium-low heat, stirring once or twice, until the cabbage is tender but still retains a touch of bite, 14 to 16 minutes.

Remove the pot from the heat and remove and discard the bay leaves. Stir in the honey, the remaining 2 tablespoons vinegar, and the butter, if desired. Season to taste with salt and pepper. Serve hot.

expo67

Roasted Carrots with Carrot-Top Pesto

Serves 4 to 6

I love carrots pretty hard, and I really get off on figuring out uses for parts of an ingredient I might normally toss. The "discovery" of using carrot tops to make pesto (I'm not the first to think of it) is a great example. The slight bitterness of the herbaceous greens is a great match for the sweet roasted carrots, but you can also use it in place of basil pesto for pasta, or to top other roasted vegetables or grilled salmon or chicken.

---

2 bunches medium carrots with tops (10 to 12 carrots)

1½ teaspoons red wine vinegar

⅓ cup plus 1½ tablespoons extra-virgin olive oil, plus more for drizzling

Kosher salt

3 tablespoons pine nuts

1 small garlic clove

½ cup finely grated Parmigiano-Reggiano (about 2 ounces)

1 cup plain whole-milk Greek yogurt

Freshly ground black pepper

Heat the oven to 425°F, with racks in the middle and lower thirds.

Leaving about 1 inch of the stems on, cut off the tops from the carrots and reserve. (The little bit of stems that you leave on the carrots, which turn crispy during roasting, are freakin' delicious. You'll thank me later.) Rinse the carrots and pat dry (don't peel). If your carrots are larger than ½ to ¾ inch in diameter at the top end, cut lengthwise in half.

Arrange the carrots on a baking sheet. Drizzle with the vinegar, 1½ tablespoons of the oil, and ½ teaspoon salt and toss to coat. Arrange the carrots in a single layer and roast on the lower oven rack until golden and tender, 25 to 30 minutes.

Meanwhile, spread the pine nuts on a small baking sheet (or in a pie pan). Toast on the middle oven rack, stirring once or twice, until lightly golden, 3 to 4 minutes. Remove from the oven, transfer the nuts to a plate, and let cool.

Pull off enough of the leaves from the carrot tops to yield 2 packed cups; wash and spin-dry.

In a food processor, pulse the garlic and toasted pine nuts to a coarse paste. Add the carrot tops, Parmesan, and ¼ teaspoon salt and pulse again to combine, scraping down the sides of the bowl once or twice. While processing, add the remaining ⅓ cup oil in a slow, steady stream. (I like to keep my pesto rather thick for this recipe and then drizzle the dish later with more olive oil. If you prefer a looser pesto, add 1 to 2 tablespoons more oil.)

When the carrots are ready, spread ¼ cup of the yogurt on a serving platter. Pile the carrots on top. Dollop with the remaining ¾ cup yogurt, then spoon the pesto on top. Drizzle with oil and sprinkle with pepper.

Cauliflower "Rice" with Parmigiano

Serves 4

When it's blitzed in a food processor, raw cauliflower becomes light and fluffy—like rice or couscous, but with lower carbs (hence its popularity). I add Parm and fresh parsley to complement its sweet, nutty flavor. Although you can now buy packages of cauliflower "rice" at some markets, ricing the cauliflower yourself takes just a minute and delivers a fresher and more robust flavor. Enjoy this as a side dish, toss into pasta or over salads, or tuck into pita sandwiches—or snack on leftovers straight from the fridge.

---

1 medium to large head cauliflower (1½ to 2 pounds), rough stem end trimmed

3 tablespoons olive oil

Kosher salt

1 cup finely grated Parmesan, preferably Parmigiano-Reggiano (about 3 ounces)

⅓ cup finely chopped fresh flat-leaf parsley

½ teaspoon freshly ground black pepper

Cut the cauliflower florets and tender stem into 1-inch pieces and place in a food processor (don't fill the bowl more than three-quarters full; work in batches if necessary). Pulse until the cauli is finely chopped into grain-like pieces. Alternatively, you can use the small holes of a box grater to rice the cauliflower.

In a large skillet, heat the oil over medium-high heat. Add the cauliflower, sprinkle with ½ teaspoon salt, and cook, stirring occasionally, until softened but with a slight bite, 5 to 7 minutes. Sprinkle with the cheese, parsley, and pepper, stir to combine, and remove from the heat. Adjust the seasoning to taste and serve.

Tip The fine shreds of cheese that you get when you use a Microplane rasp-type grater melt into this "rice" beautifully. If you don't have one, any fine grater will do.

Cauliflower Steaks

WITH TURMERIC + CRUNCHY ALMONDS

Serves 2 or 3

One day I picked up a head of cauliflower at the grocery store with no plan in mind, just a bit of faith that my pantry staples back home would inspire. Indeed they did! First, some gochujang—the savory-sweet fermented Korean chile paste. Marcona almonds for nuttiness and texture. Sticky dates for their rich caramel sweetness. This dish is vegan—great after a weekend of indulgence. Serve it with rice or your favorite grain and make it a meal. *The photo is on pages 98–99.*

CAULIFLOWER

1 large head cauliflower (about 1½ pounds)

¼ cup olive oil

2 teaspoons ground turmeric

¼ teaspoon kosher salt

4 large Medjool dates, pitted and thinly sliced lengthwise

½ cup loosely packed fresh cilantro leaves

3 tablespoons roasted salted almonds, preferably Marcona

DRESSING

3 tablespoons finely chopped tender fresh cilantro stems

2 tablespoons gochujang or Sriracha

2 tablespoons fresh lime juice (from 1 large lime)

1 tablespoon extra-virgin olive oil

1 teaspoon honey

Pinch of kosher salt

Gochujang, Korean chile paste, is available at Korean markets, many large supermarkets, and online. If you can't find it, you can substitute Sriracha here.

For the cauliflower: Heat the oven to 425°F, with a rack in the middle.

Remove and reserve any green leaves from the cauliflower, then trim and discard the rough part of the stem. Cut the cauliflower lengthwise into two or three ¾-inch-thick steak-like slices. The rest will fall apart, but that's OK—it will still taste great.

In a small bowl, whisk together the oil, turmeric, and salt. Arrange the cauliflower steaks and pieces, along with any leaves, on a baking sheet, drizzle with the oil mixture, and gently turn the cauliflower with your fingers to coat. Roast until golden and tender but not at all mushy, 25 to 30 minutes.

Meanwhile, make the dressing: In a jar with a lid or in a medium bowl, vigorously shake or whisk together all of the ingredients.

Arrange the roast cauliflower on a platter and drizzle with the dressing. Top with the dates, cilantro leaves, and almonds. Serve hot.

Cauliflower Steaks with Turmeric and Crunchy Almonds
(page 97)

Summer Corn with Chorizo + Cilantro

Serves 4

Five ingredients. Fifteen minutes. That's all this simple summer side dish takes. I enjoy a bowl solo but also serve it as a side for steak, fish, and chicken dishes. It makes a super-delicious taco filling too. The key is not to overcook the corn, so it maintains a nice plumpness and bite.

1 (7-ounce) package Spanish (dried) chorizo, cut into cubes (about 1⅔ cups)

3 ears corn, shucked and kernels cut from the cobs

½ cup coarsely chopped fresh cilantro—leaves and tender stems

½ cup finely grated Parmesan, preferably Parmigiano-Reggiano (about 2 ounces)

2 teaspoons grated lime zest

1 tablespoon plus 2 teaspoons fresh lime juice (from 1 large lime)

Kosher salt

Heat a large skillet over medium heat until very hot but not smoking. Toss in the chorizo and cook, undisturbed, until crispy on the bottom, about 5 minutes. Then continue cooking, stirring occasionally, until crispy all over, about 5 minutes more.

Add the corn and cook until it is warm and crisp-tender, 1 to 2 minutes, then stir in the cilantro, cheese, lime zest, lime juice, and a pinch of salt. Cook for 1 minute more, then remove from the heat. Adjust the seasoning to taste. Serve hot.

Tip Dried chorizo is a robust-flavored hard Spanish (or Spanish-style) pork sausage, seasoned with smoked paprika (pimentón) and other spices. It's great for cooking or simply slicing and serving with cheeses or other cured meats. Look for it in the ethnic food section or with the other cured meats at larger supermarkets, or order it online.

Tender Peas with Butter + Mint

Serves 4

If there's one takeaway from this book, it's my love for frozen peas. I eat them with abandon, steamed and tossed with canned tuna, olive oil, and lemon juice for a quick snack any day of the week. I add them to rice dishes, many of my pastas, and all sorts of other dishes, as well as sauces and stews: stroganoff, beef bourguignon, coq au vin, tagine, Bolognese, tomato sauce . . . I throw them into omelets or egg scrambles, where they add a pop of green brightness. I blitz peas into a puree or fork-mash them in a bowl with some extra-virgin olive oil and salt and eat them just like that.

If I'm missing a veg side for a Sunday meal or dinner party, all I have to do is pull a bag from the freezer. They're an old-school classic, a new-school darling, super-healthy, and so inexpensive! Here they're in one of their most simple and perfect states, and you can pair them with anything or just eat them straight from the skillet. My intro to this dish is longer than the time it takes to make 'em. You're welcome.

---

1 (16-ounce) bag frozen peas

2 tablespoons salted butter

10 large fresh mint leaves, torn

Flaky sea salt, such as Maldon

While they're still in the bag, gently squish the peas to break up large clumps. Transfer them to a large skillet, add 3 tablespoons water, and heat over medium-high heat, stirring occasionally with a wooden spoon until any still-frozen clumps are mostly broken up, 2 to 5 minutes.

Throw in 1 tablespoon of the butter and continue cooking, stirring occasionally, until the peas are bright green and tender, about 2 minutes more. Try one every now and then; you want them to remain plump (limit wrinkles, please).

Add the remaining tablespoon of butter and the mint and toss together, then season with flaky salt to taste. Serve hot.

Parsnip-Potato Puree with Butter + Chives

Serves 4

Parsnips, earthy, nutty, and sweet, look a lot like cream-colored carrots. Cooked with a bit of potato, they make a silky puree that plays well with Scallops with Carrot Butter and Crispy Capers (page 208), Cast-Iron Butter-Basted Steak (page 224), and Macadamia-Crusted Lamb Lollies with Spicy Honey Agrodolce (page 230).

2 pounds parsnips, preferably small to medium, peeled and cut crosswise into 2-inch pieces

1 small Yukon Gold potato (4 ounces), peeled and quartered

3 tablespoons unsalted butter

Kosher salt and freshly ground black pepper

2 tablespoons finely chopped fresh chives or flat-leaf parsley, or a mix

In a medium saucepan, combine the parsnips, potato, and 2 cups water. Bring just to a boil, reduce the heat to medium-low, cover, and simmer until the vegetables are very soft, 10 to 15 minutes.

Using a slotted spoon, transfer the vegetables to a food processor, reserving the cooking liquid. Add 2 tablespoons of the butter, a generous pinch each of salt and pepper, and a scant ½ cup of the reserved cooking liquid. Puree until smooth. Adjust the seasoning to taste, then fold in the herbs, leaving a little to sprinkle on top.

Transfer the puree to a serving dish and swirl decoratively with a rubber spatula. Dot with the remaining tablespoon of butter and sprinkle with the reserved herbs. Serve.

If you're going dairy-free or just prefer a lighter dish, use a good-quality extra-virgin olive oil in place of the butter. For a more rustic look and feel, mash the parsnips with a potato masher or fork instead of pureeing them.

Baby Potatoes

with Butter + Dill

Serves 4

This dish of creamy baby potatoes with bursting delicate skins, tossed in salty butter with a good dose of dill, is more than the sum of its parts. Served at room temperature, it makes a great alternative to a mayo-based potato salad, with no worries about leaving it out in the heat. You can pair it with Crispy-Skin Salmon with Horseradish Cream Sauce (page 174) or Cast-Iron Butter-Basted Steak (page 224), if you like.

1 pound baby potatoes (1 to 1½ inches in diameter; any color/variety), scrubbed

2 to 3 tablespoons coarsely chopped fresh dill (to taste)

2 tablespoons salted regular or cultured butter, cut into cubes

Flaky sea salt, such as Maldon

Salted butter seems to penetrate the skins of these hot boiled spuds better than unsalted. If you want to get really fancy, try a cultured butter, which has a higher fat content than most commercially made American butters, making it creamier and more flavorful.

Place the potatoes in a medium saucepan, add cold water to cover by 2 inches, and bring to a boil, then reduce to an active simmer. Cook until the potatoes are tender and can be easily pierced with a fork or skewer, 8 to 12 minutes, depending on their size.

Drain the potatoes in a colander, then transfer to a large bowl. Add half of the dill, half of the butter, and a good pinch of flaky salt. Gently toss until the butter is melted. Top with the remaining butter and dill and season with more salt to taste.

Serve the potatoes warm or at room temperature.

Roasted Potato Wedges with Montreal Steak Seasoning

Serves 4

It was a happy surprise for me to find Montreal Steak Seasoning (a little piece of my home) in the United States. Every Montrealer knows this blend, and although you'll find several brands in the spice section of most mainstream U.S. supermarkets, it's not as commonly known here. So I'm glad to introduce you to what might become your new favorite seasoning: a mix of spices that, along with black pepper and cayenne, often includes garlic, paprika, coriander, and dill. A great seasoning for burgers, fish, roasts, and the rim of a Bloody Mary glass, I also love it on these crispy potatoes. Roasting the spuds on a preheated baking sheet gives you ultra-golden edges without frying.

1½ pounds Yukon Gold or other yellow potatoes, cut lengthwise into ½-inch wedges

3 tablespoons olive oil

1 heaping tablespoon Montreal Steak Seasoning, such as McCormick (see headnote)

Finely chopped fresh chives for garnish (optional)

Heat the oven to 425°F, with a rack in the lower third.

Place a baking sheet (not nonstick) on the lower oven rack and heat for 10 minutes. Meanwhile, in a large bowl, toss together the potatoes, oil, and steak seasoning.

Remove the baking sheet from the oven and immediately add the potatoes, scraping any excess oil and seasoning from the bowl. Spread the potatoes out in a single layer, cut side down, and roast until the bottoms and edges of the potatoes are golden, 35 to 40 minutes.

Using a metal spatula, loosen the potatoes and toss, then continue roasting to further deepen the color and crispiness, about 5 minutes more.

Serve the potatoes hot, sprinkled with chives, if desired.

Serves 4

Roasted Sweet Potato Fries

WITH CHIMICHURRI

I love the happy accidents that occur (often out of desperation!) when I put together a few things from whatever is in the fridge or pantry and come up with a great new dish in the process. In this case, it was some leftover roasted sweet potatoes, drizzled with a little sauce from a steak dinner the night before and then sprinkled with Parm. Now it's on regular rotation in my kitchen. Tangy, garlicky chimichurri (aka Argentina's answer to pesto) is better than ketchup on sweet potato fries. Make this one for a family night or small dinner party. It's as fun to eat as it is to prepare. Chimichurri is also great drizzled over a rotisserie chicken, grilled pork chops, and shrimp.

CHIMICHURRI

1/2 cup finely chopped fresh flat-leaf parsley

1/4 cup plus 2 tablespoons extra-virgin olive oil

2 tablespoons finely chopped shallots or red onion

2 tablespoons red wine vinegar

1 small garlic clove, finely chopped

1/2 teaspoon red pepper flakes

1/4 teaspoon kosher salt

FRIES

3 pounds sweet potatoes (not peeled—healthy!)

1/4 cup olive oil

1/2 teaspoon kosher salt

1/3 cup finely grated Parmesan, preferably Parmigiano-Reggiano (about 1 ounce)

Freshly ground black pepper

Let the freshly made sauce sit at room temperature for at least 15 minutes, or up to an hour, to allow the flavors to develop.

For the chimichurri: In a medium bowl, stir together all of the ingredients. Let stand at room temperature to let the flavor of the sauce develop while you make the fries, or for up to 1 hour.

For the fries: Heat the oven to 450°F, with racks in the middle and upper thirds. Heat two 13-x-18-inch baking sheets (not nonstick) in the oven for 10 minutes.

Meanwhile, cut the sweet potatoes into sticks about ½ inch wide and 2 to 4 inches long, depending on the size of your potatoes. In a large bowl, toss the potatoes with the oil and salt.

Arrange the sweet potatoes in a single layer on the hot baking sheets. Roast, rotating the sheets and switching their positions on the racks halfway through, until the potatoes are golden and cooked through, 20 to 22 minutes.

Sprinkle the potatoes with the Parm and pepper and drizzle with a few tablespoons of the chimichurri. Serve with the rest of the sauce on the side for dipping.

Frenchified Latkes with Chive Sour Cream

Makes about 2 dozen 2-inch latkes

You don't have to be Jewish to love these crispy potato pancakes! I French mine up by adding nutty Comté or Gruyère cheese and serve them with big spoonfuls of chivey sour cream.

CHIVE SOUR CREAM

1 cup (8 ounces) full-fat sour cream

2 tablespoons finely chopped fresh chives, plus more for sprinkling

Finely grated zest of 1/2 lemon

Pinch of kosher salt

LATKES

2 pounds russet (baking) or Yukon Gold potatoes

1 medium sweet or yellow onion

1 cup coarsely grated Gruyère, Comté, or Emmenthaler (about 4 ounces)

1 large egg, beaten

2 teaspoons chopped fresh thyme

Kosher salt

1/2 teaspoon freshly ground black pepper

Neutral oil, such as canola, for shallow-frying

For the chive sour cream: In a small bowl, stir together all of the ingredients.

For the latkes: Heat the oven to 200°F. Line a plate with paper towels.

Peel the potatoes, then coarsely grate. Do the same with the onion. Wrap the vegetables together in a clean kitchen towel and squeeze out all the water.

In a large bowl, stir together the potato mixture, cheese, egg, thyme, ¾ teaspoon salt, and the pepper.

In a large skillet, heat ¼ inch of oil over medium-high heat until shimmering. (You can test the heat with a shred of potato before you begin frying; when the oil is ready, the potato shred will sizzle and bubble on contact.) Working in batches, spoon about 2 tablespoons of the potato mixture into the pan for each latke, gently pressing down with a spatula to flatten them. Reduce the heat to medium and fry, turning once, until the latkes are golden and crisp on both sides, about 3 minutes per side. Transfer to the paper towels to drain, then season with salt. Place on a baking sheet and keep warm in the oven while you fry the remaining batches.

Serve the latkes warm with the sour cream and chives on the side.

Tangy Beluga Lentils

Serves 4

Lentils are quick enough for weeknight cooking, healthy, filling, and, most important, delicious. Belugas are my favorite variety, named for their shiny black color and beady resemblance to caviar. (The name is also so elegant to say.) This dish goes with everything, and it keeps well for several days. Enjoy as a side or combine it with chopped kale, sliced hot dogs, or even an oozy egg. Think meal prep, guys!

---

1 cup (about 7 ounces) beluga lentils, rinsed and picked over

1/3 cup finely chopped fresh flat-leaf parsley, plus 3 leafy sprigs

1 garlic clove, gently smashed but not peeled

1 bay leaf

3 tablespoons extra-virgin olive oil

1 small carrot, finely diced

1 celery stalk, finely diced

1/4 cup finely diced onion

Kosher salt and freshly ground black pepper

3 tablespoons apple cider vinegar

1 teaspoon Dijon mustard

In a medium saucepan, combine the lentils, parsley sprigs, garlic, and bay leaf. Add water to cover by 2 inches and bring just to a boil, then reduce the heat and simmer uncovered until the lentils are tender yet still a touch firm to the bite, 18 to 20 minutes.

Meanwhile, in a medium skillet, heat 1 tablespoon of the oil over medium heat. Add the carrot, celery, and onion and cook, stirring occasionally, until tender yet still a touch firm to the bite, 5 to 7 minutes. Transfer to a large bowl and stir in a pinch each of salt and pepper. Set the skillet aside.

Just before the lentils are ready, stir together the vinegar, the remaining 2 tablespoons oil, the Dijon, ½ teaspoon salt, and a generous pinch of pepper in the skillet and heat over low heat just until warm to the touch (do not simmer or boil), 1 to 2 minutes. Remove from the heat.

Drain the lentils. Discard the parsley, garlic, and bay leaf. Add the warm lentils, warm vinaigrette, and chopped parsley to the bowl of vegetables and stir to combine. Adjust the salt and pepper to taste. Serve warm or at room temperature.

Tip You can substitute any small variety of lentil that holds its shape when cooked, such as French Le Puy lentils.

expo67

Frida
Georgia
Yayoi
Artemisia
Louise

SOUPS AND STEWS

Serves 4

Easy Bastardized Ramen

No, this isn't the soup you get in real ramen shops. But I have to say, the flavor is pretty great! Store-bought miso paste and chili garlic sauce give a kick of umami. The toppings can be mixed and matched to your liking, depending on what's fresh and available at your market. Since the broth freezes beautifully, I often make a few batches at once, which means I can enjoy ramen on weeknights.

SOUP BASE

3 garlic cloves, sliced

Kosher salt

1 tablespoon plus 1 teaspoon toasted sesame oil

½ pound ground pork

2 medium carrots, julienned or grated

4 scallions, thinly sliced, whites and greens kept separate

1½ tablespoons grated peeled fresh ginger

2 teaspoons chili garlic sauce (see Tip)

8 cups low-sodium chicken broth

TO ASSEMBLE/SERVE

4 large eggs

16 ounces fresh or 10 ounces dried ramen, soba, or udon noodles

¼ cup miso paste (white, red, or yellow)

2 tablespoons unsalted butter, cut into bits

Toasted sesame oil

Chili garlic sauce

Optional toppings: 1 sheet nori, quartered and cut into strips; bean sprouts, sunflower sprouts, or microgreens; thawed frozen corn; toasted sesame seeds; and/or chopped fresh cilantro

For the soup base: Mound the garlic with ¼ teaspoon salt on a cutting board. Using a chef's knife, mash and chop together into a paste. Set aside.

In a large Dutch oven or other wide heavy pot, heat 1 tablespoon of the sesame oil over medium heat. Add the pork and ½ teaspoon salt and cook, stirring frequently and breaking up the meat with a wooden spoon, until the pork is cooked through, about 2 minutes.

Tip

Chili garlic sauce is a spicy, tangy Asian chili paste that goes with all sorts of dishes and is a great all-purpose hot sauce. Indonesian sambal oelek is similar, but without the garlic. Sriracha is a pureed and slightly sweeter version. All of these sauces are sold in ethnic food shops and big supermarkets, and online, and you can often use them interchangeably.

Continues

The eggs, plus a dab of butter, are the keys to the richness that makes this such a satisfying meal!

Transfer the pork to a plate. Add the remaining teaspoon of sesame oil to the pot, then add the carrots, scallion whites, half of the scallion greens, and ⅛ teaspoon salt. Cook over medium heat, stirring occasionally, until the carrots are tender, 2 to 3 minutes.

Push the vegetables aside to clear a space in the center of the pot. Add the ginger, chili garlic sauce, and reserved garlic paste to the cleared space and cook for 30 seconds, stirring constantly. Stir in the pork and any accumulated juices, then add about ¼ cup of the broth. Scrape up the browned bits from the bottom of the pot, then add the remaining broth, increase the heat to high, and bring just to a boil, skimming any foam from the top. Remove from the heat. Adjust the salt to taste. (*The soup base can be cooled, covered, and refrigerated for up to 3 days or frozen for up to 3 months.*)

To assemble and serve: Pour boiling water into four large soup bowls to heat them. Set aside. Bring a pot of water to a boil for the noodles.

Meanwhile, bring a medium saucepan of water to a gentle simmer. Gently lower the eggs into the water and cook for 6 minutes. Using a slotted spoon, transfer the eggs to a bowl filled with ice water. Set aside.

Add the noodles to the pot of boiling water and cook according to the package instructions. Drain and set aside.

Heat the soup base just to a boil, then remove from the heat. Add the miso and butter and stir until the miso is fully dissolved. Cover to keep warm.

Peel the eggs and cut in half. Drain the hot water from the serving bowls, then divide the noodles among them. Ladle the hot soup over the top. Top with the egg halves, the remaining scallion greens, a drizzle of sesame oil, and the added toppings of your choice, including more chili garlic sauce if you want a kick of heat.

Chilled Beet Soup

WITH PICKLES + DILL (CHLODNIK)

Serves 4

This could be considered Poland's version of gazpacho. In a cuisine that doesn't fear fried pork chops, lard, and potatoes, its freshness is a welcome change. Chlodnik (pronounced *hwahd-nihk*), meaning "a little cold something" or "the cooler," is a stunning magenta, flecked with crunchy vegetables and pickles, with a swirl of sour cream. Though pickles in soup might sound strange, they add bright flavor. This dish was a family mainstay when I was growing up, enjoyed on many hot summer afternoons in our backyard in Montreal. *The photo is on pages 118–119.*

---

1 (10-ounce) bottle borscht concentrate (see Tip)

4 cups low-sodium vegetable broth

1 cup (8 ounces) full-fat sour cream

4 large eggs

¾ cup cubed (¼-inch) cucumber

Kosher salt

¾ cup cubed (¼-inch) dill pickles

½ cup finely chopped fresh dill

6 small or 4 medium radishes, thinly sliced

3 tablespoons finely chopped fresh chives or scallions

In a bowl, whisk together the borscht concentrate, broth, and half of the sour cream until smooth. Add ½ cup ice cubes and refrigerate, covered, for a couple of hours, until cold. (*The soup base can be prepared up to 3 days ahead and kept covered and refrigerated.*)

Meanwhile, fill a medium saucepan with water and bring to a simmer. Using a slotted spoon, gently lower the eggs into the water, taking care not to drop them into the pan. Cook for exactly 10 minutes, then transfer the eggs to a bowl of ice water and let cool for about 5 minutes. Drain the eggs and refrigerate, covered, until you're ready to serve the soup. (*The shell-on eggs can be refrigerated for up to 5 days.*)

To assemble the soup: Peel the eggs and quarter or halve each one. Toss together the cucumber and ⅛ teaspoon salt in a bowl.

Divide the pickles, cucumbers, and half of the dill among four soup bowls. Ladle the chilled soup into the bowls. Top with the eggs, radishes, chives or scallions, and the remaining dill and sour cream. Serve immediately.

Tip I urge you to go the extra mile to track down borscht concentrate, which is super flavorful and can be found at Polish markets and online; it's simply concentrated beet juice with salt and natural spices. Instead, you can substitute two 24-ounce bottles of borscht, available at most larger grocery stores, and omit the veg broth.

Chilled Beet Soup with Pickles and Dill (Chlodnik; *page 117***)**

Roasted Butternut Squash Soup

WITH GINGER + LIME

Serves 4

My middle sister, Aleksandra, first made a puree like this for me when I was a picky kid who refused to eat his veg. Roasting the squash caramelizes it, and lime juice and peppery dried chile perk things up.

---

5 cups ½-inch cubes peeled, seeded butternut squash (from a 2½-pound squash)

2 medium carrots, chopped into ¼-inch pieces (about 1½ cups)

¼ cup extra-virgin olive oil

Kosher salt

1 medium onion, coarsely chopped (about 1½ cups)

2 tablespoons finely chopped tender fresh cilantro stems (optional)

2 tablespoons grated peeled fresh ginger

1 garlic clove, finely chopped

1 tablespoon grated lime zest (from 1 to 2 large limes)

2 teaspoons honey

4 cups low-sodium chicken or vegetable broth

2½ tablespoons fresh lime juice (from 1 to 2 large limes)

½ cup full-fat sour cream

½ cup roasted salted cashews, coarsely chopped

Coarsely chopped fresh cilantro for garnish (optional)

Red pepper flakes for sprinkling (optional)

Heat the oven to 425°F, with a rack in the middle.

Put the squash and carrots on a baking sheet and toss with 2 tablespoons of the oil and ¾ teaspoon salt. Roast, stirring once halfway through, until lightly golden in spots and the carrots are crisp-tender, 25 to 30 minutes. Remove from the oven.

In a large Dutch oven or other wide heavy pot, heat the remaining 2 tablespoons oil over medium heat. Add the onion and cilantro stems, if using, and cook, stirring occasionally, until the onion is golden, 10 to 12 minutes. Add the ginger, garlic, lime zest, honey, and ¾ teaspoon salt and stir for 1 minute, then add the roasted vegetables.

Add a splash of the broth and scrape the bottom of the pot with a wooden spoon to release all of the golden bits. Add the remaining broth and 1 cup water, increase the heat to high, and bring just to a boil. Reduce to a simmer and cook the soup until the flavors come together, 7 to 10 minutes.

Working in batches, carefully puree the soup in a blender until smooth. *(The soup can be refrigerated for up to 5 days. If you're making it ahead, wait until you've reheated it before adding the lime juice; it loses its oomph when reheated.)* Stir in the lime juice, then adjust the salt to taste.

Ladle the soup into bowls. Swirl 2 tablespoons sour cream into each bowl. Sprinkle with the cashews. Finish with cilantro, if using, and a pinch of red pepper flakes.

Five-Onion Soup with Crispy Shallots

Serves 4 to 6

This recipe was inspired by my junior high school years, in West Virginia, when my family belonged to a country club called Glade Springs. After tennis practice, I would go to the resort's restaurant and order the onion soup. It was rich, creamy, and divine. One day a waiter asked me if I'd like to put the order on my parents' tab. Clever teen that I was, I said, "Sure!" and then proceeded to enjoy the soup three times a week for a month, until my father received a very unwelcome bill. But it was totally worth his ensuing wrath. Caramelized roasted onions blitzed with heavy cream is the soup equivalent of my spirit animal.

CRISPY SHALLOTS

1 cup thinly sliced shallots (about 2 large)

½ cup neutral oil, such as canola

Kosher salt

SOUP

2 medium sweet onions, such as Vidalia, coarsely chopped

1 large white onion, coarsely chopped

1 small red onion, coarsely chopped

1 tablespoon olive oil

Kosher salt

2 medium leeks, white and light green parts only, cut lengthwise in half and then into ¼-inch-wide half-moons

4 tablespoons (½ stick) unsalted butter

1 garlic clove

2 teaspoons coarsely chopped fresh thyme, plus more for serving

¼ cup Cognac or other brandy

4 cups low-sodium beef broth

¾ cup dry white wine

1 cup heavy cream

Freshly ground black pepper

Using a variety of onions results in a complexity of flavor that you don't get with just one type.

For the crispy shallots: Combine the shallots and oil in a small skillet (not nonstick) and cook over medium-low heat, stirring occasionally, until golden brown, 18 to 22 minutes; pay close attention toward the end of the cooking time, when they will quickly become golden. Remove from the heat.

Using a slotted spoon, transfer the shallots to a fine-mesh sieve set over a bowl. Let drain for 5 to 10 minutes, then transfer the shallots to paper towels, season generously with salt, and set aside (the shallots will continue to crisp as they sit).

For the soup: Heat the oven to 400°F.

Put the sweet onion, white onions, and red onion on a large baking sheet and toss with the oil and ¾ teaspoon salt. Roast, stirring once halfway through, until the onions are tender and golden, 14 to 16 minutes.

Meanwhile, wash the leeks well and pat dry. In a large saucepan, melt the butter over medium heat. Add the leeks, garlic, thyme, and ½ teaspoon salt and cook, stirring occasionally, until the leeks are tender, 12 to 15 minutes (do not brown). Add the Cognac or other brandy and cook until the liquid is mostly evaporated, about 5 minutes. Remove the pan from the heat.

In two batches, combine the roasted onions, leek mixture (set the pan aside), and 1 cup of the broth in a blender or food processor. Pulse until the mixture is mostly smooth, with a few chunky bits. Transfer to the pan, stir in the wine, ½ teaspoon salt, and the remaining broth, and bring to a simmer over medium-high heat. Stir in the heavy cream, bring just to a simmer, and remove from the heat. Adjust the salt to taste.

Serve the soup hot, topped with the crispy shallots, fresh thyme leaves, and pepper to taste.

The Polish Hangover Soup (ZUREK)

Serves 6 to 8

This tangy, fortifying soup has brought millions of Poles back to life after a hard night of bad decision-making (read: vodka). The healing quality comes, ostensibly, from a fermented sour rye soup starter called *zakwas*. Though you can buy it at Polish markets, it takes just a few minutes to mix it up yourself. Just build in a few days to your soup-making plan for the fermentation to take place. The hearty combination of root vegetables, kielbasa, pickles, sour cream, and hard-boiled eggs makes this soup a meal.

ZAKWAS

1/2 cup rye flour

2 garlic cloves, finely chopped

1 bay leaf

SOUP

1/3 pound thick-cut smoked bacon, cut crosswise into 1/4-inch-wide pieces

2 medium onions, coarsely chopped

2 1/2 pounds kielbasa or bratwurst, cut into 1/2-inch-thick slices

1 large carrot, halved lengthwise and cut into 3/4-inch-thick slices

1 large parsnip, quartered lengthwise and cut into 3/4-inch-thick slices

1 medium celery root, peeled and cut into 1/2-inch cubes

8 sprigs fresh flat-leaf parsley, plus finely chopped fresh parsley for garnish

3 fresh or dried bay leaves

2 teaspoons dried marjoram

1/8 teaspoon ground allspice

Kosher salt

1/4 cup drained prepared horseradish

1/4 teaspoon freshly ground white pepper

GARNISH

Sour cream

3 or 4 hard-boiled eggs (for 1/2 egg per serving; see page 117), peeled and halved

2 cups coarsely chopped dill pickles (about 4 medium)

Chopped fresh dill or parsley

continues

915 Manhattan Avenue
Brooklyn, NY 11222
Tel. (718) 389-6149

For the zakwas: Pour 2 cups boiling water into a heatproof 1-quart jar or glass bowl. Let cool to warm.

Stir the flour, garlic, and bay leaf into the warm water. Tightly cover/seal the jar or bowl with plastic wrap (use a rubber band or two to hold the wrap tightly) and let sit in a warm, dark place (like a cupboard) for 4 to 5 days; "burp" the mixture every 2 days by removing the plastic wrap to let the air out, then resealing it again (this will prevent a little culinary explosion). Alternatively, you can seal the jar or bowl with cheesecloth (more breathable), held tightly with a rubber band, and you will not have to burp the mixture.

The zakwas is ready when it has a pungent fragrance, a solid, spongy deposit on top, and a light brown-gray liquid at the bottom. Scrape off any green or moldy bits that appear on the top (a healthy sign of the fermentation process and not dangerous!), and remove and discard the bay leaf. Strain the zakwas through a sieve into a bowl; discard the solids. You'll have about 1½ cups liquid. Use however much you have; the exact amount is not important.

For the soup: In a large Dutch oven or other wide heavy pot, cook the bacon over medium-high heat, stirring occasionally, until golden and crisp, 5 to 7 minutes. Using a slotted spoon, transfer to a medium bowl. Add the onions to the pot and cook, stirring occasionally, until tender and lightly golden, 12 to 14 minutes. Transfer to the bowl with the bacon. Add the kielbasa or bratwurst to the pot and cook, stirring occasionally, until golden brown, 12 to 15 minutes. Transfer to the onion mixture. Pour off and discard the fat from the pot.

Add the carrot, parsnip, celery root, parsley sprigs, bay leaves, marjoram, allspice, 1 teaspoon salt, and 7 cups water to the pot, bring to a simmer, and cook until the vegetables are almost tender but with a little bite, 12 to 15 minutes.

Add the zakwas, horseradish, and onion mixture to the pot, return the soup to a simmer, and cook until the vegetables are tender and the broth is flavorful, 10 to 12 minutes. Stir in the white pepper. Season to taste with salt. Remove and discard the parsley sprigs and bay leaves.

Spoon the soup into bowls. Top each bowl with a big dollop of sour cream, a hard-boiled egg half, the chopped pickles, and some dill or parsley, and serve.

Rich Turkey Chili with Dark Beer + Chocolate

Serves 6 to 8

I've made this so many times for my BFF Reema Sampat that she now calls it her own. The day I discovered that chocolate and beer add a rich, malty depth to the warm, spicy flavors of chili was a life-changing one, in the culinary sense. This is a one-pot situation that's great for parties. The chili also freezes well, so you can make big batches ahead and have it at the ready.

⅓ pound thick-cut bacon, cut crosswise into ¼-inch-wide strips

2 pounds ground turkey, preferably dark meat

Kosher salt

2 tablespoons olive oil

2 medium onions, coarsely chopped (about 3 cups)

1 red bell pepper, cored, seeded, and cut into small cubes

3 tablespoons tomato paste

5 garlic cloves, finely chopped

1 canned chipotle chile in adobo, seeded and finely chopped (about 2 teaspoons), plus 2 tablespoons of the adobo sauce

2 teaspoons dried oregano

¾ teaspoon ground cumin

2 (15-ounce) cans black beans, rinsed and drained

1 (14-ounce) can crushed tomatoes (fire-roasted or plain)

1 (12-ounce) bottle dark beer (ideally Guinness; Negra Modelo is good too)

1½ cups low-sodium chicken broth

2 ounces dark chocolate, coarsely chopped (scant ½ cup)

2 tablespoons apple cider vinegar

2 teaspoons molasses (not blackstrap) or packed dark brown sugar

For serving: Sliced avocado, chopped fresh cilantro, pickled jalapeños, grated cheddar, diced white onion, lime wedges, and/or Greek yogurt or sour cream

In a large Dutch oven or other wide heavy pot with a lid, cook the bacon over medium-high heat, stirring occasionally, until crisp and golden, 5 to 7 minutes. Using a slotted spoon, transfer the bacon to a large bowl. Cook the turkey in the remaining bacon fat over high heat, stirring frequently and breaking up the meat into small bits with a wooden spoon, until cooked through, about 5 minutes. Season with 1½ teaspoons salt, then transfer the turkey and any juices to the bowl with the bacon.

continues

To save the rest of an opened can of chipotles in adobo, scoop small mounds onto a parchment-lined baking sheet and freeze until firm (4 to 6 hours). Transfer to a zipper-lock freezer bag and keep frozen until ready to use. You can use the chipotles straight from the freezer.

Heat the oil in the same pot over medium-high heat. Add the onions and bell pepper and cook, stirring occasionally, until the veg are softened and the onions are golden, about 8 minutes. Stir in the tomato paste and garlic and cook for 1 minute, stirring, then stir in the chipotle and adobo sauce, oregano, cumin, and 2 teaspoons salt. Cook until fragrant, about 2 minutes, then add the beans, crushed tomatoes, beer, broth, chocolate, and turkey mixture. Bring to a gentle simmer and cook, uncovered, stirring occasionally, until the chili is deeply flavorful, about 1 hour and 15 minutes.

Remove the pot from the heat and stir in the vinegar and molasses or brown sugar. Adjust the seasoning to taste. Serve hot, with your favorite accompaniments.

Pomegranate-Walnut Chicken Stew

(FESENJAN)

Serves 4 to 6

This alluring Persian stew, called fesenjan, is typically prepared during the winter solstice holiday Shab-e Yalda, but it's also a great dinner party or, really, anytime dish. I love the way the warming spices and tangy pomegranate molasses and juice combine to produce a rich, tart sauce. Ground walnuts add toasty notes and thicken the dish. I generally make fesenjan with chicken, though duck is also common. Serve Rice and Potato Tahdig with Saffron and Turmeric (page 154) or a bowl of steamed long-grain rice alongside.

---

1 cup (about 3½ ounces) walnut pieces

2 pounds boneless, skinless chicken breasts, cut into 1½- to 2-inch cubes

Kosher salt

2½ tablespoons olive oil

2 medium onions, finely chopped (about 3 cups)

1 tablespoon tomato paste

2 teaspoons packed light or dark brown sugar

½ teaspoon ground turmeric

¼ teaspoon ground cinnamon

1 cup low-sodium chicken broth

1 cup pomegranate juice

½ cup pomegranate molasses

Pomegranate seeds for garnish (optional)

Chopped fresh parsley or cilantro for garnish (optional)

Heat the oven to 350°F, with a rack in the middle.

Spread the walnuts on a baking sheet and bake until fragrant and lightly toasted, about 8 minutes. Transfer to a plate and let cool completely, then pulse in a food processor to finely chop (do not make a paste). Set aside.

Season the chicken with 1½ teaspoons salt. In a large Dutch oven or other wide heavy pot with a lid, heat the oil over medium-high heat. Working in two or three batches (taking care not to crowd the pot), brown the chicken until lightly golden on all sides, 5 to 7 minutes. Transfer the browned pieces to a plate as you go. Set aside.

Continues

Pomegranate molasses, a thick, concentrated syrup made by reducing pomegranate juice, adds a fruity tang to both sweet and savory dishes. (It's also great as a flavoring for club soda or other bubbly water!) It's available at health food stores, ethnic markets, and larger supermarkets.

Add the onions to the pot and cook, stirring occasionally, until softened and golden, about 10 minutes. Push the onions to the edges of the pot to clear a space in the center. Add the tomato paste, brown sugar, turmeric, and cinnamon to the cleared space, quickly stirring the mixture until fragrant, about 30 seconds. Add the chicken, with any accumulated juices, and broth and, using a wooden spoon, scrape any browned bits from the bottom of the pot. Stir in the pomegranate juice, pomegranate molasses, and walnuts. Increase the heat to high and bring the liquid just to a boil, then reduce to a gentle simmer. Partially cover and simmer until the sauce is dark brown and slightly thickened, 20 to 25 minutes.

Uncover the pot and continue cooking until the sauce is thickened and has turned a deep mahogany brown, about 10 minutes more.

Remove from the heat and adjust the seasoning to taste.

Serve the stew garnished with pomegranate seeds and parsley or cilantro, if desired.

Boeuf Bourguignon

with Parsnips + Cognac

Serves 6 to 8

I have Julia Child—via Meryl Streep, who played her in the movie *Julie & Julia*, and Amy Adams, who played the famous blogger Julie Powell—to thank for this one. They inspired me to master this OG French comfort stew. It's actually quite easy and a real crowd-pleaser. I mix in some parsnips along with the carrots, because I like the earthy sweetness they lend to the dish. Marinating the beef in wine overnight (or for at least 8 hours) is way worth it, enhancing both the flavor of the beef and the rich red wine notes. Serve this with a side of buttery mashed potatoes or a warm crusty baguette for sopping up the magical sauce.

Tip Before cutting the bacon, toss it in the freezer for 10 to 15 minutes, which will make it easier to slice into neat, even pieces.

3 pounds boneless beef chuck, cut into 1½- to 2-inch pieces

1 large onion, finely chopped

2 medium carrots, unpeeled, cut into ¾-inch-thick rounds

2 medium parsnips, unpeeled, cut into ¾-inch-thick rounds

3 garlic cloves, gently smashed and peeled

10 sprigs fresh thyme, tied together with kitchen twine

2 bay leaves

1 (750-ml) bottle rich red Burgundy or Pinot Noir

Kosher salt and freshly ground black pepper

½ pound thick-cut bacon, cut crosswise into ½-inch-wide pieces

¼ cup all-purpose flour

⅓ cup Cognac or other brandy

Place the beef, onion, carrots, parsnips, garlic, thyme, and bay leaves in a large bowl. Add the wine. Refrigerate, covered, for at least 8 hours, or overnight.

Remove the beef from the marinade and pat thoroughly dry on paper towels. Using a slotted spoon, transfer the carrots and parsnips to a bowl; set aside. Reserve the marinade and aromatics.

Generously season the beef with salt and pepper. In a large Dutch oven or other wide heavy pot with a lid, cook the bacon over medium-high heat, stirring occasionally, until crisp, 8 to 10 minutes. Using a slotted spoon, transfer to paper towels to drain. Working in batches (do not crowd the meat), brown the beef on all sides in the hot bacon fat, 7 to 9 minutes. Transfer to a bowl as you go.

continues

Return all the beef and the bacon to the pot. Sprinkle in the flour and cook over medium heat, stirring constantly, for 3 minutes to cook out the raw taste of the flour. Add the Cognac or other brandy and cook, scraping up the browned bits from the bottom of the pot with a wooden spoon, until the liquid is mostly evaporated, about 3 minutes. Add the reserved marinade, with the bay leaves and thyme, and 2 cups water and bring just to a boil. Reduce the heat to low, cover, and cook for 2½ hours.

Add the reserved carrots and parsnips and cook until the beef is very tender and the vegetables are tender but with a little bite, 30 to 45 minutes more. Remove and discard the thyme and bay leaves, and skim off some of the fat before serving. (*The stew, which gets better as it sits, can be made up to 3 days ahead, cooled, covered, and refrigerated. As it chills, the fat rises and solidifies, so you can easily lift it off and discard. Reheat over low heat.*)

Serves 6 to 8

New-Style Polish Hunter's Stew

(Bigos Revisited)

Name a more iconic winter stew than bigos. I'll wait . . .

OK, fine, so unless you're Polish, you've probably never heard of this, but that's about to change. Every member of my family and all the friends in my parents' social circle each had their own version of this meat, kraut, and cabbage stew, along with endless debate as to the best mix of ingredients to include. My version uses prunes, which impart a subtle caramel-like sweetness, and wine in place of the traditional beer, for a little French influence. (In a perfect world, I'd suggest letting the stew sit for a day or three in the fridge before serving, to enhance the flavors even more.) Serve this with rye bread slathered with cold salty butter, and you'll feel a little Polish—I promise.

1 cup (1 ounce) dried porcini or other wild mushrooms

1/2 pound thick-cut bacon, cut crosswise into 1/2-inch-wide pieces

1 pound kielbasa, cut into 1/4-inch-thick slices

1 pound Polish kabanos (see Tip) or other smoky dried pork sausage, cut into 1-inch-thick slices, or an extra 1/2 pound kielbasa

1 pound boneless pork loin, cut into 1-inch cubes

1 medium onion, coarsely chopped (about 1 1/2 cups)

1 (1-pound) green cabbage, halved, cored, and cut crosswise into 1-inch-wide strips

Kosher salt

1 (32-ounce) jar or bag sauerkraut, drained (4 cups)

3 bay leaves

1 tablespoon finely chopped fresh marjoram or 1 1/2 teaspoons dried

1/2 teaspoon ground allspice

4 cups low-sodium beef broth

2 cups Bordeaux or other dry, fruity red wine

3/4 cup pitted prunes, cut in half

Rye bread and cold salted butter for serving (optional)

Tip Kabanos is a smoked and air-dried Polish sausage, typically seasoned with black pepper, garlic, caraway, and allspice. It is used for both cooking and snacking. A "gourmet" beef or pork stick will work as a substitute, as long as it doesn't have added flavors like barbecue or chipotle.

continues

In a small bowl, combine the dried mushrooms and 2 cups hot water; set aside.

In a large Dutch oven or other wide heavy pot with a lid, cook the bacon over medium-high heat until golden and crispy, about 5 minutes. Using a slotted spoon, transfer the bacon to a large plate. Add the kielbasa and kabanos or other sausage and cook, stirring occasionally, until the meat is golden and crispy, 8 to 10 minutes. Transfer the sausages to the plate with the bacon. Add the pork loin to the pot and cook, stirring occasionally, until cooked through, about 6 minutes. Transfer the pork to the plate with the bacon and sausages.

Add the onion to the fat left in the pot and cook over medium heat until crisp-tender, about 3 minutes. Add the cabbage and cook until the vegetables are softened, 6 to 8 minutes.

Meanwhile, lift the mushrooms from the soaking liquid and transfer to a plate. Reserve 1 cup of the liquid.

Stir ½ teaspoon salt into the cabbage mixture, then add the sauerkraut. Make a well in the center of the pot, add the bay leaves, marjoram, allspice, drained mushrooms, and sausage mixture, and cook until fragrant, about 2 minutes. Add the beef broth, wine, prunes, and reserved mushroom broth and stir well. Then reduce to a gentle simmer and cook, covered, stirring occasionally, getting into the edges of the pot with the spoon, for 30 minutes.

Uncover and continue cooking until the liquid is reduced a bit and the stew is flavorful, about 45 minutes more.

Remove and discard the bay leaves. Serve hot, with rye bread and butter, if desired.

STAUB

PASTA AND RICE

Baked Turkey, Mac, and Cheese

Serves 8

When I was young and my parents went out, they would leave my sisters in charge of feeding me, and we'd often indulge in Kraft Mac & Cheese, with ground meat mixed in. I loved the light sharpness of the Day-Glo orange "cheese" sauce and the tubular pasta it coated. In my baked version, a blend of three cheeses forms a rich, complex sauce. I always go for extra-crispy bites from the corners of the baking dish after finishing my plate. (I guess this still brings out the kid . . .) A heap of arugula dressed with fresh lemon juice and good olive oil makes it a complete meal. *The photo is on pages 144–145.*

Tip Italian Fontina is best for both cooking and eating, because of its rich, nutty flavor and super-creamy texture. The Swedish and Danish types, though they cost less, pale in comparison.

BAKE

Kosher salt

1½ cups coarsely grated extra-sharp cheddar (about ⅓ pound)

1½ cups coarsely grated Fontina, preferably Italian (about ⅓ pound)

1½ cups coarsely grated Gruyère or Emmenthaler (about ⅓ pound)

1 tablespoon extra-virgin olive oil

1 small onion, finely chopped (about 1 cup)

1 pound ground turkey, preferably dark meat

Freshly ground black pepper

¼ cup finely chopped fresh flat-leaf parsley

1 (16-ounce) box cavatappi or macaroni (elbow) pasta

3¾ cups whole milk

9 tablespoons (1 stick plus 1 tablespoon) unsalted butter, plus more for greasing

¼ cup plus 2 tablespoons all-purpose flour

¼ teaspoon cayenne pepper

⅛ teaspoon freshly grated nutmeg

½ cup heavy cream

¾ cup panko bread crumbs

SALAD

5 ounces baby arugula (10 loosely packed cups)

2 tablespoons extra-virgin olive oil

1 tablespoon fresh lemon juice

Kosher salt

For the bake: Heat the oven to 350°F, with a rack in the middle. Butter a 9-x-13-x-2-inch baking dish or 3-quart gratin dish.

Bring a large pot of water to a boil and salt it 'til it tastes like the ocean (taste it). In a medium bowl, gently mix together the three cheeses; set aside.

In a large skillet, heat the oil over medium-high heat. Add the onion and cook, stirring occasionally, until translucent, about 5 minutes. Add the turkey and ¾ teaspoon salt and cook, breaking up the meat into small bits with a wooden spoon, until cooked through, 4 to 5 minutes. Stir in ¼ teaspoon pepper and 2 tablespoons of the parsley. Remove the pan from the heat.

Cook the pasta in the boiling water for 2 minutes less than the lowest cooking time recommended on your package. Drain the pasta and set aside. Set the pot aside.

In a small saucepan or a microwavable bowl, gently warm the milk over low heat or for 10-second intervals just until hot to the touch. Remove from the heat.

Add 6 tablespoons of the butter to the pot you used for the pasta and melt over low heat. Add the flour and cook, whisking frequently, until the mixture is foamy and bubbling, about 5 minutes. Stir in the cayenne, nutmeg, ¼ teaspoon salt, and ⅛ teaspoon pepper, then whisk in ½ cup of the hot milk (the mixture may seize up); continue whisking until the mixture is fairly smooth. Continue adding the milk ½ cup at a time, whisking constantly, getting into the edges of the pot, until all the milk is incorporated and the sauce is thickened and smooth, 3 to 4 minutes total. Sprinkle in 2 cups of the cheese mixture, stirring as you go, and then stir just until the cheese is melted and the sauce is smooth, about 1 minute. Remove the sauce from the heat and stir in the pasta and 1 teaspoon salt.

Sprinkle ½ cup of the reserved cheese evenly into the baking dish. Spoon about half of the pasta on top. Top with the turkey and 1 more cup of the cheese, then cover with the remaining pasta and then the remaining cheese. Pour the cream over the top.

Melt the remaining 3 tablespoons butter in a medium skillet over medium heat. Stir in the panko to coat, then sprinkle the mixture evenly over the pasta.

Bake until the cheese sauce is bubbling and the crust is golden, 40 to 45 minutes. Remove from the oven and let sit for 10 minutes.

Meanwhile, make the salad: In a large bowl, toss together the arugula, oil, lemon juice, and a pinch or two of salt.

Sprinkle the bake with the remaining 2 tablespoons parsley and serve hot, with the salad alongside.

Baked Turkey, Mac, and Cheese
(page 142)

Mac and Cheese with Fresh Herbs + Peas

Serves 4 to 6

After a challenging day, or for those times when I decide to fully ignore my efforts to be health-conscious, mac and cheese is the perfect source of a delightful food coma. And since there's no roux or baking involved, this is the version I turn to when time is as tight as my patience. Tangy goat cheese and Parm flavor the creamy sauce, while peas add a little sweetness. They also fit adorably into the orecchiette (aka "little ears") pasta.

Kosher salt

1 (16-ounce) box orecchiette or small pasta shells

1½ cups frozen peas

1½ cups grated Parmesan, preferably Parmigiano-Reggiano (5 ounces), plus more for serving

5 ounces soft goat cheese, at room temperature

½ cup heavy cream or half-and-half

½ cup finely chopped mixed fresh herbs, such as basil, tarragon, mint, and/or chives or scallion greens

Freshly ground black pepper

Bring a large pot of water to a boil and salt it 'til it tastes like the ocean (taste it). Add the pasta and cook until it is about 2 minutes under al dente. Stir in the peas and cook for 1 to 2 minutes more. Scoop out and reserve ½ cup of the pasta cooking water, then drain the pasta and peas.

While the pasta is cooking, in a large heatproof bowl, stir together the Parmesan, goat cheese, cream or half-and-half, and ½ teaspoon salt until smooth.

Stir ¼ cup of the reserved pasta cooking liquid into the cheese mixture, then add the pasta and peas and about half of the herbs. Toss to combine. Add more pasta cooking liquid if the sauce seems dry.

Spoon the pasta into serving bowls. Top with the remaining herbs, more Parm, and pepper to taste.

Bucatini Cacio e Pepe

Serves 2 or 3

Two things: cheese and pepper. That's pretty much the Italian name of this pasta, and it is one of the best. Technique here is everything. The pasta cooking liquid is a key ingredient, and the trick is to make it extra starchy (which helps bind the sauce) by using less water than you normally do to cook your noodles. Mixing the cheese with some of that starchy hot liquid before adding it to the pan also helps the sauce emulsify.

---

1 cup finely grated (ideally, use a Microplane grater so that it's thin) Pecorino Romano (2 ounces), plus more for serving

Kosher salt

1/2 pound bucatini or spaghetti

1 1/4 teaspoons coarsely ground black pepper, plus more for serving

3 tablespoons extra-virgin olive oil

Set out two or three serving bowls. Place the cheese in a small heat-resistant bowl near the stove.

Fill a large wide pot or deep skillet with water to come up 3 inches. Bring the water to a boil and salt it 'til it tastes like the ocean (taste it). Add the pasta and cook, stirring occasionally, for 2 minutes less than the lowest cooking time recommended on your package.

Meanwhile, in a large skillet, heat the pepper in the oil over low heat just until the oil is warm to the touch and the pepper is fragrant, 1 to 2 minutes. Remove the pan from the heat and set aside.

About 1 minute before the pasta is ready, scoop out ¼ cup of the pasta cooking water and add it to the cheese, stirring to make a thick paste. Ladle about ¼ cup of the boiling pasta cooking water into each of the serving bowls to warm them.

Scoop out another ½ cup or so of cooking water and reserve. Drain the pasta and transfer to the skillet with the oil and pepper. Toss over low heat for 1 minute to coat the pasta with the oil and cook off most of the excess liquid. Remove the pan from the heat and add ⅓ cup of the reserved pasta cooking liquid to the pasta. Add the cheese paste, stirring well. Add more of the pasta cooking liquid by the tablespoonful if necessary, until you have a creamy sauce that coats each strand of pasta.

Drain the water from the pasta bowls, add the pasta to the bowls, and serve immediately, topped with more cheese.

Tip The black pepper is central to this dish, which is why you want to use a very coarse grind and do the grinding just before making the pasta. If you don't have a great pepper mill, place whole peppercorns on a cutting board and use the bottom of a heavy skillet (using a pressing and rocking motion) to coarsely crack them.

Summer Pasta Salad

WITH PICKLED GRAPES

Serves 4 to 6

A good pasta salad offers a mix of zippy ingredients, such as fresh tomatoes, briny olives, or a citrusy dressing—the high notes—and ones that anchor the dish, like cheese, mayo, or a yogurt sauce—the low notes. I use quick-pickled grapes, seasoned with coriander and shallot, in tandem with sweet corn, fresh basil, and smoky Gouda cheese. The result has just the right balance. Bonus: This dish holds up well at picnics, barbecues, and other multi-hour entertaining situations.

Kosher salt

1 cup orzo

1½ teaspoons extra-virgin olive oil

¾ cup red wine vinegar

⅓ cup sugar

1 large shallot, finely chopped (about ½ cup)

1 teaspoon coriander seeds

2 cups stemmed seedless green grapes, halved

1 pint (about 2 cups) cherry, grape, or Sunburst tomatoes, or a mix, halved

1½ cups fresh corn kernels (from 3 ears)

5 ounces smoked Gouda, cut into ¼-inch cubes (1 heaping cup)

2 cups loosely packed fresh basil leaves, large leaves torn

Freshly ground black pepper

Bring a medium pot of water to a boil and salt it 'til it tastes like the ocean (taste it). Add the orzo and cook until al dente; drain. Transfer to a large bowl, toss with the oil, and set aside to cool. (*The orzo can be refrigerated for up to 1 day. Bring to room temperature before continuing.*)

Meanwhile, in a small saucepan, bring the vinegar, sugar, and ¼ teaspoon salt just to a boil, stirring until the sugar is dissolved. Transfer to a small heatproof bowl, add the shallot and coriander seeds, and let cool, about 20 minutes.

Add the grapes to the brine. Let stand, gently stirring once or twice, until pickled, about 20 minutes.

Drain the pickled grape mixture (discard the brine) and add to the bowl with the orzo. Add the tomatoes, corn, cheese, and basil and gently stir to combine. Season with salt and pepper to taste. (*The salad, except for the basil, can be refrigerated, covered, up to 8 hours ahead. Bring to room temperature and toss with the basil before serving.*)

Serves 4 to 6

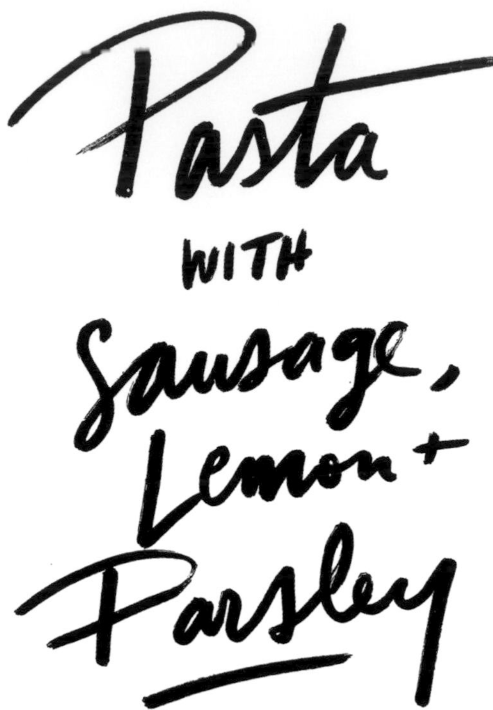

This weeknight pasta can double as an impressive dish for entertaining. Lightly toasting then crushing a few whole fennel seeds emphasizes the flavors of the Italian sausage while adding a lively freshness. Be sure to brown the sausage well for nice crispy edges—it tastes so good that way.

1 teaspoon fennel seeds

Kosher salt

1 pound trumpet pasta, garganelli, campanelle, or other short tubular pasta

1 tablespoon olive oil

1 pound sweet Italian sausage, casings removed

½ cup medium-dry white wine, such as Pinot Gris or Pinot Grigio

1 packed tablespoon grated lemon zest (from 2 large lemons)

¼ cup fresh lemon juice (from 2 large lemons)

3 tablespoons cold unsalted butter, cut into bits

1 cup coarsely grated Parmesan, preferably Parmigiano-Reggiano (3 ounces), plus more for serving

¾ cup coarsely chopped fresh flat-leaf parsley

Coarsely ground black pepper

In a small dry skillet, toast the fennel seeds over medium-low heat, shaking the pan back and forth, until the seeds are fragrant and lightly toasted, 1 to 2 minutes. Transfer to a cutting board and let cool, then crush with a mortar and pestle or the bottom of a heavy pot. Set aside.

Bring a large pot of water to a boil and salt it 'til it tastes like the ocean (taste it). Add the pasta and cook until it's about 2 minutes under al dente.

Meanwhile, in a large skillet, heat the oil over medium-high heat until very hot but not smoking. Add the sausage and cook, breaking up the meat into small pieces with a wooden spoon, until deeply golden in spots, about 6 minutes. Add the wine and cook, scraping up any browned bits on the bottom of the pan, until about half of the liquid is evaporated, 1 to 2 minutes. Add the lemon zest and juice. Whisk in the butter one piece at a time, just until melted and incorporated, to form a nice silky sauce.

Scoop out ¾ cup of the pasta cooking water and reserve. Drain the pasta and return it to the pot. Add the cheese, ½ cup of the reserved pasta cooking water, ½ teaspoon salt, and the fennel seeds. Quickly toss everything together to coat the pasta, adding more of the pasta cooking liquid if the dish appears dry, then stir in the parsley. Adjust the seasoning to taste.

Serve immediately, topped with pepper and a sprinkling of more cheese.

Serves 4 as a main dish, 6 as a first course

Risotto was the meal I made most often for friends when I was a broke university student in Montreal. With little more than some Arborio rice, chicken broth, Parm, and an add-in or two, I had an impressive homemade meal. As time has passed, my add-ins have gotten a little more luxe. Enter this classic, which I was first inspired to make when I had some leftover bubbly from a party the night before. While Champagne is nice, less expensive bubbles, like cava or Prosecco, or any good dry white wine, is perfectly fine. You can build a fuller meal around this by serving it after an appetizer such as Roasted Carrots with Carrot-Top Pesto (page 94), or as a starter before Rosemary Pork Tenderloin (page 228) or Chile-Maple Roasted Chicken (page 216).

I like a slightly soupy-style risotto, referred to in Italian as *all'onda* (meaning "wavy"), rather than a drier version. You'll know it's ready when there's just enough liquid in the pan for the cooked rice to ripple yet still have a thick, creamy consistency.

---

7 cups low-sodium chicken broth

4 tablespoons (1/2 stick) unsalted butter

1 cup finely chopped onion

Kosher salt

1½ cups Arborio or Carnaroli rice

1½ cups Champagne or other sparkling or dry white wine

¾ cup finely grated Parmesan, preferably Parmigiano-Reggiano (about 3 ounces), plus more for serving

1 tablespoon grated lemon zest

1½ tablespoons fresh lemon juice

Freshly ground black pepper

In a medium saucepan, bring the broth to a simmer over medium heat. Reduce the heat to low.

In a large heavy saucepan, melt the butter over medium heat. Add the onion and ½ teaspoon salt and cook, stirring frequently, until the onion is translucent and softened, 8 to 10 minutes (do not let brown). Add the rice and cook, stirring constantly, until it turns opaque, about 4 minutes. Add the Champagne or wine, increase the heat to medium-high, and cook, stirring constantly, until it has evaporated.

Tip A wooden spatula that's wide and flat at the bottom is the tool I like for stirring risotto because it allows you to stir and fold the rice while scraping the bottom and sides of the pan as you go.

Add ¾ cup of the hot broth and cook, stirring frequently yet gently and getting into the edges of the pot (mixing too roughly will eventually break the grains, which you want to avoid), until the broth is absorbed. Continue adding broth ¾ cup at a time, allowing it to be absorbed each time before adding more, until the rice is tender yet still firm to the bite and the risotto is creamy and still slightly soupy, 16 to 18 minutes total. (You may have some broth left over.)

Remove the pan from the heat. Add the cheese, lemon zest, and lemon juice and stir until the cheese is melted, then season with salt and pepper to taste.

Spoon the risotto into bowls and top with more Parm and pepper. Serve immediately.

Rice + Potato Tahdig

WITH SAFFRON + TURMERIC

Serves 6

This aromatic Persian rice dish is named for the golden, crispy layer, known as tahdig, that forms at the bottom of the pot as the rice slowly steams—it's the part that everyone wants to scoop out when it's served. My version contains potato and is flecked with chopped parsley and dried cranberries. It's fun for dinner parties and delicious with roast chicken and fish, or alongside other veg dishes. It's a perfect match for Pomegranate-Walnut Chicken Stew (Fesenjan; page 131). This takes a while to cook. It's worth it.

---

2 cups basmati rice

Kosher salt

1/4 teaspoon crumbled saffron threads

4 tablespoons (1/2 stick) unsalted butter

3/4 teaspoon ground turmeric

1 small russet (baking) or Yukon Gold potato, peeled and thinly sliced into rounds (about 1/16 inch thick)

1 tablespoon coarsely chopped fresh flat-leaf parsley

1 tablespoon dried cranberries, coarsely chopped

Sumac for sprinkling (optional)

Place the rice in a large bowl. Add 1 tablespoon salt and cold water to cover by 1 inch and stir, then let stand for 30 minutes. Drain the rice in a strainer and rinse under cold water until the water runs clear.

Meanwhile, in a large bowl, combine the saffron with 1 tablespoon hot water; set aside.

Place the rice in a large saucepan. Add 8 cups water and 2 tablespoons salt and bring to a boil over high heat, then reduce the heat to a simmer and cook, uncovered, until the rice is slightly softened on the outside, 3 to 4 minutes. Drain the rice in a sieve and rinse under cold running water, then shake well to remove excess water. Set aside.

Cut out a round of parchment paper to cover the bottom of a 10-inch-wide or other wide heavy pot with a lid, such as a Dutch oven. Line the pan with the parchment round. Add 2 tablespoons butter and melt over medium-low heat, then remove from the heat and stir in the turmeric and ¼ teaspoon salt. Arrange the potatoes, overlapping, on the bottom of the pan.

Continues

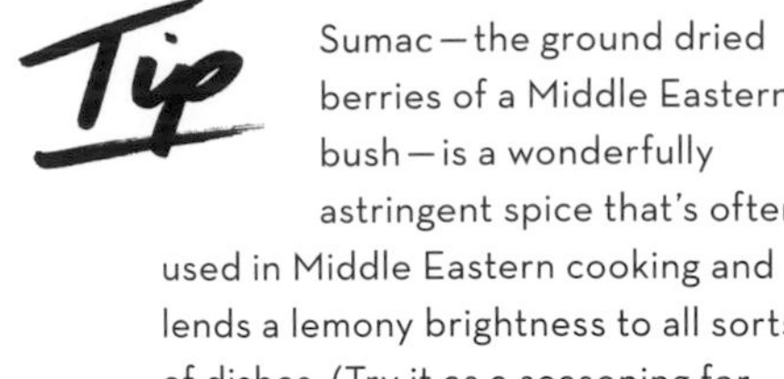

Sumac—the ground dried berries of a Middle Eastern bush—is a wonderfully astringent spice that's often used in Middle Eastern cooking and lends a lemony brightness to all sorts of dishes. (Try it as a seasoning for chicken or fish, or sprinkle it over hummus.) Look for it at specialty grocers or online.

Add the rice and ¼ teaspoon salt to the bowl with the saffron water and gently stir to combine. Spoon the rice on top of the sliced potatoes (do not press or pack down) and, using a fork, gently spread the rice in an even layer. Cook, uncovered, over medium heat, until the mixture is fragrant, about 10 minutes. Wrap a clean dishcloth around the lid and tightly cover the pan, folding the cloth over the edges of the lid. Reduce the heat to the lowest possible setting and cook, undisturbed, until the potatoes are crisp (you can peek by lifting up the mixture at an edge or two with a large serving spoon), 1½ to 1¾ hours. Uncover and dot with the remaining 2 tablespoons butter.

Remove the pan from the heat. Invert the dish onto a serving plate, then lift off and discard the parchment paper. Sprinkle with the parsley, cranberries, and sumac, if using. Serve.

Tomato, Basil + Melty Mozzarella Baked Rice

(Sartu di Riso)

Serves 8 to 10

I was completing a treadmill session at the gym when, switching TV channels, I landed on a Food Network segment that featured my favorite Giada De Laurentiis, beaming her megawatt smile as she demonstrated how to make a traditional *sartu di riso* with her auntie. It's a big cheesy dish of rice molded around a filling of thick tomato and basil sauce that's baked in a Bundt pan—kinda like a veg version of the magnificent pasta timpano in the classic movie Big Night! I've since made my version both for holidays and anytime entertaining.

---

2 tablespoons olive oil, plus more for brushing and drizzling

1 cup finely chopped onion

1 cup finely chopped carrots

1 celery stalk, finely chopped

2 garlic cloves, finely chopped

4 bay leaves

Kosher salt

1 tablespoon tomato paste

2 (28-ounce) cans whole tomatoes, preferably San Marzano, with their juices

1 small bunch fresh basil, plus whole leaves for garnish

1 cup finely grated Parmesan, preferably Parmigiano-Reggiano (about 3 ounces), plus a Parm rind, if you have one, and more grated cheese for serving

2½ cups Arborio rice

5 cups low-sodium chicken or vegetable broth

2 large eggs, lightly beaten

2 tablespoons unsalted butter, softened, for the pan

1 cup Italian-style seasoned bread crumbs

1 (8-ounce) ball fresh mozzarella

Heat the oil in a large saucepan over medium-high heat. Add the onion, carrots, and celery and cook, stirring occasionally, until the onion is translucent but not browned, about 5 minutes. Add the garlic, 2 of the bay leaves, and a pinch of salt, then stir in the tomato paste and cook until the paste begins to caramelize, about 2 minutes.

Continues

Add the tomatoes and their juices, breaking the tomatoes apart with a wooden spoon. Then bury the bunch of basil and the Parmesan rind, if using, in the sauce. Reduce the heat to low and simmer, uncovered, until the sauce has thickened and the flavors have developed, about 30 minutes. Remove and discard the Parm rind (if you used it) and the basil. Set the sauce aside to cool.

Meanwhile, in a large pot, combine the rice, broth, and the remaining 2 bay leaves. Bring just to a boil over high heat, reduce to a gentle simmer, cover, and cook, without removing the lid, for 15 minutes. The rice should be al dente. Give the rice a stir, transfer it to a large bowl, and let cool until it's just warm to the touch, 10 to 15 minutes.

Heat the oven to 400°F, with a rack in the middle.

Stir the grated Parm into the cooled rice. Adjust the salt if necessary (it should taste nicely seasoned), then stir in the eggs to thoroughly combine.

Generously grease the inside of a 12-cup Bundt pan, including the central tube, with all the butter. Add ¾ cup of the bread crumbs, then tilt the pan to coat all sides. Using your hands, line the bottom and sides of the pan, including the central tube, with an even layer of the rice, using about three quarters of it and bringing it up to about ½ inch from the top of the pan. Tear the mozzarella into small shreds and scatter over the bottom layer of rice. Add all but about 1 cup of the tomato sauce, then cover with the remaining rice, smoothing the top with the back of a spoon to seal the edges. Top with the remaining ¼ cup bread crumbs and brush them with oil (which will give you a nice crispy crust).

Bake until the top is golden brown and the edges are crispy, 30 to 35 minutes. Remove from the oven and let cool on a wire rack for 10 minutes. Meanwhile, gently rewarm the reserved sauce.

Invert the rice onto a large serving plate. Fill the cavity with the reserved tomato sauce. Garnish with basil leaves, then top with more grated Parm and a drizzle of oil. Slice into wedges and serve immediately.

STAND BY ME™

WEEKNIGHT HEALTHY-ISH

Aussie Breakfast for Dinner Sammie

Serves 4

This egg sammie may look like any other egg sandwich out there, but it's got a special something that makes it extra-delicious and very Aussie: Vegemite. A thick dark-brown yeast paste that's packed with nutrients ("for vitality," the package says, and many doctors agree it's one of the world's richest sources of B vitamins and more), the umami spread is an Aussie toast classic that also finds its way into many other dishes. Its salty, malty, and slightly meat-smoky notes balance the richness of the avocado and eggs here, while seasoning the dish with a flavor that's at once familiar (the salty part) and unique (the meaty-malty part). Quick, easy, super-satisfying, and healthy, this sammie is both breakfast and dinner in my home.

2 tablespoons olive oil

4 large eggs

4 slices rustic country loaf or sourdough bread, toasted

2 tablespoons unsalted butter, softened

1 to 2 teaspoons Vegemite (or more, for the pros out there!)

1 avocado, halved, pitted, peeled, and thinly sliced

1⅓ loosely packed cups microgreens, mâche, or baby greens

½ teaspoon red pepper flakes

Flaky sea salt, such as Maldon, or kosher salt

Heat the oil in a large nonstick skillet over medium-high heat until very hot but not smoking. One at a time, crack the eggs into the skillet. Cook until the oil begins to pop and bubble at the edges of the eggs, 3 to 4 minutes. Reduce the heat to low, cover the skillet, and continue cooking until the whites are fully set and the edges are golden brown, about 1½ minutes more.

Meanwhile, smear the toast with the butter and then the Vegemite, going easy on the Vegemite if you're a rookie. (You'll work up to adding more gradually.) Top with the avocado and then the greens.

Top the sandwiches with the warm fried eggs and, using the tines of a fork, scrape the egg yolks a bit, just until they start to run. Sprinkle with the red pepper flakes and salt. Serve immediately.

Marmite is Vegemite's British cousin, and though the Brits and Aussies argue about which one is king, a side-by-side taste test is the best way to gauge your fave. I tend to reach for Vegemite, but you can use them interchangeably here.

French Omelette with Cheese + Chives

Serves 1

I'm not one to shy away from a good American omelet, where the eggs are fully cooked and often browned along the edges—the kind you find in diners and brunch spots across the country. But the moment I learned how to make a true French omelette—the delicate, slightly wet sort that's more like a soft, warm pillow—I learned what omelette dreams are really made of. This dish easily becomes a complete meal if served alongside your favorite salad. Whether you're cooking for yourself on a weeknight or want to impress a date the morning after, it's as easygoing as it is romantic.

Buy the very best eggs you can for this dish, opting for farm fresh from your local farmers' market if you can. You deserve to know what this tastes like when the yolks are rich in both color (deep orange, not Peep-yellow, is what you're looking for) and flavor, as those purchased locally most often are.

Tip A French omelette is said to be 10 percent ingredients and 90 percent technique. If you fail at your first attempt to make this recipe, *ne t'inquiète pas* (don't worry!), as we say *en français;* you'll simply have a lovely pan of scrambled eggs on your hands. And once you've mastered it, you can try all kinds of good variations, adding things like cooked spinach, crispy mushrooms, and the like.

2 large eggs

2½ tablespoons unsalted butter, preferably European-style or cultured

Flaky sea salt, such as Maldon, or kosher salt

⅓ cup coarsely grated Gruyère, sharp cheddar, or Italian Fontina (about 1 ounce)

Freshly ground black pepper

1 tablespoon finely chopped fresh chives

Whisk the eggs in a medium bowl until well combined and smooth, taking care not to whip in much air. The point is to combine the yolks and whites very well.

Heat 1 tablespoon of the butter in an 8-inch nonstick skillet over medium-low heat until the butter has melted and just begins to foam. Pour in the eggs. Working quickly, gently move the pan in a circular motion over the heat (this will keep the eggs moving and evenly cooking) while you use a small rubber spatula in your other hand to stir the eggs in a loose figure-eight pattern to create small curds, scraping down the side of the skillet as you go. Continue until the eggs are mostly cooked through but just a little runny on top, 2 to 3 minutes.

Remove the pan from the heat and sprinkle the omelette (now it can be called one!) with a pinch of salt, then sprinkle the cheese down the center of the exposed egg. Gently shake the pan so that the omelette shifts toward the side of the pan opposite the handle and up the side of the pan.

The part of the omelette above the edge of the pan should fold over on itself—use your rubber spatula to give it a hand, if it doesn't. Slide 1 tablespoon butter underneath the omelette that's still in the pan. (This will help keep the omelette tender and soft—and it tastes really good.)

Using the spatula, roll up the omelette, then flip it seam side down onto a warm serving plate. Slide the remaining dab of butter (½ tablespoon) across the top, then sprinkle with a pinch each of salt and pepper and the chives. Serve hot.

REBEL
CUTS

Chickpea Masala

Serves 4 to 6

My best friend Arjun, who lived two doors down from us when I was a kid, had the luxury of a private chef who prepared incredibly delicious Indian food. I'd often sneak in an early after-school dinner at his house before going home. With just a few basic items, you can put together this bowl of chickpea goodness from that part of the world.

2 tablespoons extra-virgin olive oil

2 tablespoons unsalted butter

2 medium onions, finely chopped (about 3 cups)

4 garlic cloves, thinly sliced

2 tablespoons finely chopped peeled fresh ginger

1½ teaspoons ground coriander

1¼ teaspoons ground cumin

½ teaspoon ground turmeric

⅛ teaspoon cayenne pepper

Kosher salt

1 (28-ounce) can whole tomatoes, preferably San Marzano, with their juices

2 (15-ounce) cans chickpeas, rinsed and drained

⅓ cup dried apricots, thinly sliced

FOR SERVING

½ cup finely chopped fresh cilantro leaves and tender stems

½ cup finely chopped red onion

Lime wedges

Plain yogurt (optional)

Cooked basmati or jasmine rice (optional)

Heat the oil and butter in a Dutch oven or other wide heavy pot over medium-low heat until the butter is melted. Add the onions, garlic, and ginger and cook, stirring occasionally, until the onions are softened, about 5 minutes. Add the spices and 1 teaspoon salt.

Add the tomatoes, with their juices, and ½ cup water. Using a large wooden spoon, break up the tomatoes, then add the chickpeas and use the spoon to mash about a quarter of them. Stir in the apricots, increase the heat to high, and bring just to a boil. Reduce the heat and simmer, stirring occasionally, until slightly thickened, 18 to 22 minutes. Adjust the salt and remove from the heat.

Serve the masala hot, with the cilantro and red onion sprinkled over the top, and lime wedges on the side. Dollop with yogurt and serve with rice, if desired.

Dried apricots, while not classic, lend a welcome tang and touch of sweetness.

Serves 4

Rainy-Day Grilled Cheese

WITH PROSCIUTTO + EASY TOMATO BISQUE

This old-school pairing has turned many a long, rough day for me into bliss at first bite. Adding prosciutto to the sandwich and a sprinkling of sumac to the soup is my way of elevating the classic (you can use lemon zest if you don't have sumac). If you're a good planner, the soup can be made ahead, and then it's just a quick warm-up and 10 minutes to make the sandwiches.

BISQUE

2 tablespoons extra-virgin olive oil

1 medium onion, coarsely chopped (about 1½ cups)

Kosher salt

4 garlic cloves, finely chopped

1 (28-ounce) can whole tomatoes, preferably San Marzano, with their juices

3 cups low-sodium chicken broth

¼ cup heavy cream or half-and-half

½ teaspoon sumac or grated lemon zest

1 cup loosely packed fresh basil leaves, large leaves torn

Freshly ground black pepper (optional)

GRILLED CHEESE

¼ cup plus 2 tablespoons mayonnaise

Eight ¾-inch-thick slices brioche loaf or challah

2 cups grated extra-sharp cheddar (about ¼ pound)

4 slices (about 2½ ounces) prosciutto

4 tablespoons (½ stick) unsalted butter

Tip Leave your cheese in the fridge until you're ready to grate so that it stays cold. This works especially well for cheeses like cheddar that tend to easily crumble and get a bit pasty if they're at room temp when grated.

For the bisque: In a medium saucepan, heat the oil over medium heat. Add the onion and 1 teaspoon salt and cook, stirring occasionally, until translucent, 5 to 7 minutes. Stir in the garlic and cook for 1 minute. Add the tomatoes, with their liquid. Using a wooden spoon, break up the tomatoes, then add the broth and 1 teaspoon salt, increase the heat to high, and bring to a boil. Reduce to a simmer and cook for 10 minutes, stirring once or twice. Remove the pan from the heat.

Using a regular blender or immersion blender, carefully puree the hot soup (in batches if necessary) until creamy and smooth. Return to the pan if you used a regular blender. Stir in the cream and sumac or lemon zest. Adjust the seasoning to taste. Cover to keep warm.

continues

For the grilled cheese: Spread the mayo on one side of each bread slice. (This both flavors the sandwich and serves as a nice binder for the cheese.) Sprinkle about half of the cheese on 4 of the bread slices. Lay 1 prosciutto slice over each cheese-sprinkled bread slice, then top with the remaining cheese. Top with the remaining bread slices, mayo side down.

In a large skillet, melt 2 tablespoons of the butter over medium heat. Add 2 sandwiches. Gently press down with a slightly smaller flat pan lid or a large metal spatula to help brown the sammies and get the cheese nice and melty. Flip when the bottom is browned, 2 to 3 minutes, and continue cooking until the other side is golden, 2 to 3 minutes more. Transfer the grilled cheeses to a wire rack and repeat with the remaining butter and sandwiches.

Cut the sandwiches in half on a diagonal, because that is the only way to cut a sandwich and I will not hear otherwise. Serve alongside the tomato bisque, which you've just garnished with torn fresh basil and pepper, if desired. Don't forget to dip!

BEING YOURSELF,
ANIMALS,
CALLING YOUR MOTHER,
RANDOM ACTS OF KINDNESS,
DREAMING,
BELIEVING IN SOMETHING,
RECYCLING,
BEAUTY SLEEP,
NO PHONES AT THE TABLE,
WORKING HARD,
SAVING THE PLANET,

Serves 2 as a main dish, 4 to 6 as a snack

This dish is like that friend who fits into any social situation. It's a ten-minute, super-satisfying, one-pan pantry meal. Serve it for lunch or a light supper, or as a snack with crackers. Or make it without the tuna to include as part of a spread. Butter beans are probably my favorite legume—decadent, creamy, and oversized, they hold up well in the rich tomato sauce. Do use the celery leaves if you can: They wake up all the flavors.

¼ cup plus 2 tablespoons tomato paste

⅓ cup extra-virgin olive oil, plus more for drizzling

2 tablespoons finely chopped fresh dill

1 heaping tablespoon finely chopped fresh oregano, or ½ teaspoon dried

1 tablespoon fresh lemon juice

2 teaspoons honey

2 (15.5-ounce) cans butter beans, rinsed and drained

1 (5-ounce) can oil-packed tuna, drained

Flaky sea salt, such as Maldon, or kosher salt

Freshly ground black pepper

½ cup celery leaves from the heart of the bunch (optional)

Crackers for serving (optional)

Tip This recipe comes together lightning fast, so make sure to have all of your ingredients ready to go when you begin preparing it.

In a small skillet, whisk together the tomato paste and oil and heat over medium heat, stirring constantly, until the oil is bubbling and the tomato paste begins to break down, 1 to 2 minutes. Stir in the dill, oregano, lemon juice, and honey, reduce the heat to medium-low, and cook, stirring constantly, until the flavors come together, 3 to 5 minutes. (The oil will remain slightly separated; this is OK.) Remove from the heat and let stand until slightly cooled, about 3 minutes.

In a bowl, gently stir together the sauce, beans, tuna, ½ teaspoon flaky salt or ¼ teaspoon kosher salt, and a generous pinch of pepper. Transfer to a serving bowl, drizzle with oil, and top with a generous pinch of salt and the celery leaves, if using. Enjoy on its own or with your favorite crackers.

Farro Bowl

with Sweet Potatoes, Arugula + Chicken

Serves 4 to 6

During my days as assistant to Ted Allen and his husband, Barry, I tended to a wide variety of business, including preparing lunches. Ted will tell you that this dish remains his favorite of all the things I ever made for him. The idea sprang from my desire to cut ties with quinoa (delicious, but omnipresent at the time) and create a dish that could be noshed on long after I had gone for the day. The key here, for maximum weeknight enjoyment, is to do your meal prep ahead and have the mixed chicken, sweet potato, and farro base, as well as the accompaniments, in the fridge, as I did for Ted and Barry. Then you can put a bowl together in mere minutes when you want it.

1½ pounds sweet potatoes, cut into ½-inch cubes

¼ cup olive oil

¾ teaspoon chili powder

¼ teaspoon cayenne pepper

Kosher salt

1 cup farro, semipearled or pearled (or "10-minute farro"; see Tip)

3 tablespoons apple cider vinegar

2 bay leaves

1 pound boneless, skinless chicken breasts

¼ cup fresh lemon juice (from 2 to 3 large lemons)

1 cup coarsely chopped fresh cilantro or mint

Freshly ground black pepper

4 cups (2 ounces) loosely packed baby arugula

½ cup roasted salted almonds, preferably Marcona, coarsely chopped

1 tablespoon grated lemon zest

1 cup plain Greek yogurt

Extra-virgin olive oil for drizzling

Lemon wedges for serving

Tip

Trader Joe's sells a "10-minute farro" that is quite good and ready in half the time it takes to cook the semipearled or pearled varieties you find in most other markets.

Heat the oven to 450°F, with a rack in the lower third.

Put the sweet potatoes on a baking sheet and toss with 2 tablespoons of the oil, the chili powder, cayenne, and ¼ teaspoon salt. Spread the potatoes out in a single layer, leaving space between them (this will help make them crispy), and roast until the undersides are golden, 15 to 18 minutes. Toss with a spatula and continue roasting until crispy all over, 8 to 10 minutes more. Remove from the oven and let cool to warm or room temperature.

Meanwhile, fill a medium saucepan halfway with water (about 8 cups). Bring to a boil, then add the farro, vinegar, bay leaves, and 1½ teaspoons salt and cook until the farro is al dente (tender, but with a nice bite), 20 to 35 minutes, depending on the variety. (If you're using the TJ brand, follow the cooking time on the package.)

Meanwhile, pat the chicken dry and season with ½ teaspoon salt. Heat the remaining 2 tablespoons oil in a large nonstick skillet over medium-high heat. Add the chicken and cook, undisturbed, until lightly golden on the underside, 5 to 7 minutes. Flip and continue cooking until cooked through, 5 to 7 minutes more. Add the lemon juice to the skillet and let cook for 1 minute more, then remove the pan from the heat. Transfer the chicken to a cutting board, reserving the pan juices, and let rest for 5 minutes, then cut into ¾-inch cubes.

Drain the cooked farro, spread on a large plate or baking sheet, and let cool to warm or room temp.

In a large bowl, gently toss together the farro, sweet potatoes, chicken, the reserved pan juices, and the cilantro. Spoon the mixture into large serving bowls. Top each with a heap of arugula, a sprinkle of almonds and lemon zest, a spoonful of yogurt, a drizzle of extra-virgin olive oil, a squeeze of lemon, and salt to taste.

Serves 4

Crispy-Skin Salmon

with Horseradish Cream Sauce

Salmon is one of the most popular fish, but its delicious and nutrient-rich skin is underappreciated. This technique cooks the flesh perfectly with a contrasting crisp skin that crackles with good fats and a rich, somewhat smoky flavor. I enjoy the fish first and save the crisp part for last.

HORSERADISH CREAM SAUCE

1 cup Greek yogurt, preferably whole-milk

1/3 cup grated fresh or thoroughly drained (excess liquid squeezed out) prepared white horseradish (from a 6-ounce jar)

2 tablespoons finely chopped fresh chives, dill, or flat-leaf parsley

1 teaspoon white wine vinegar or fresh lemon juice

1/2 teaspoon kosher salt, or to taste

1/4 teaspoon cayenne pepper, or to taste

SALMON

4 (5- to 6-ounce) skin-on salmon fillets, preferably center-cut, 3/4 to 1 inch thick at the thickest part

Kosher salt

All-purpose flour for dusting

2 tablespoons neutral oil, such as canola

Tip A fish spatula is worth owning. Its springy, flexible blade allows you to press evenly on fillets or steaks without applying too much pressure and easily sneaks between the pan and anything that's delicate, so there's less chance of tearing all that crackly goodness you've worked to achieve.

For the horseradish cream sauce: In a bowl, stir together all the ingredients plus 1 tablespoon water. Adjust the salt and cayenne to taste (you can also add more horseradish, if you want extra kick). Cover and refrigerate until ready to use. (*The sauce can be made up to 1 day ahead.*)

For the salmon: Heat the oven to 225°F.

Gently pat the salmon fillets between double layers of paper towel to thoroughly dry on both sides. Season the fish all over with 1 teaspoon salt, then dust the skin side with flour, removing any excess with the back of a clean dry spoon.

In a large skillet, heat 1 tablespoon of the oil over medium-high heat until very hot but not smoking. Reduce the heat to medium-low and add 2 salmon fillets, skin side down. Using a metal spatula, press down on the fillets (move your spatula as needed to press on all of the fillets; this will keep the skin from curling and ensure an even crisp). Continue pressing, without checking on or moving the fillets (yes, this is the patience part!), until the fat is rendered from the skin and the skin is crispy, 6 to 7 minutes. Turn the fillets and cook on the flesh side for 30 seconds to 2 minutes (a quick "kiss," as chefs say), depending on

thickness, for medium-rare. Transfer the fish to a baking sheet and keep warm in the oven. Wipe out the skillet with a couple of paper towels and repeat with the remaining tablespoon of oil and fish.

Transfer the fish to serving plates and serve with the horseradish cream sauce.

Serves 4

During my few years living in West Virginia when I was a teenager, good seafood was hard to come by. You can imagine my family's delight when we discovered a market-style restaurant in the heart of the state's capital, Charleston, where one of the specialties was blackened swordfish steak with golden fried hushpuppies and honey butter. My rendition is easier and healthier, since the polenta is ready-made and the "hushpuppies" are baked, not fried, and topped with juicy burst tomatoes.

---

4 (6-ounce) swordfish steaks, 1 to 1½ inches thick

2 tablespoons butter, softened

1½ tablespoons honey

1 (18-ounce) log precooked polenta, cut into ½-inch-thick rounds

3 tablespoons olive oil

Kosher salt

¾ pound cherry tomatoes on the vine or 1 pint (about 2 cups) cherry or grape tomatoes

2 tablespoons blackened seasoning (Chef Paul Prudhomme's is my fave, or try Zatarain's)

¼ cup torn fresh basil leaves

Heat the oven to 450°F. Let the fish stand at room temperature for 10 to 20 minutes to take the chill off.

In a small bowl, stir together the butter and honey until smooth.

Put the polenta on a baking sheet and gently toss with 1 tablespoon of the oil and ¼ teaspoon salt. Arrange the polenta in a single layer on one side of the baking sheet. Brush the tops with the butter mixture. Roast for 8 minutes.

Meanwhile, in a bowl, toss the tomatoes with 1 tablespoon oil and ⅛ teaspoon salt.

Remove the baking sheet from the oven. Arrange the tomatoes on the empty side, return the pan to the oven, and roast until the polenta is lightly golden and the tomatoes are golden and beginning to burst, 16 to 18 minutes.

Meanwhile, pat the fish dry with paper towels, then sprinkle all over with the blackened seasoning and a generous pinch of salt.

Heat the remaining tablespoon of oil in a very large skillet over medium-high heat until very hot but not smoking. Place the swordfish in the pan and cook, without disturbing it, until the underside is golden, about 4 minutes. Turn the fish and cook until opaque and cooked through, 3 to 4 minutes more.

Arrange the fish, polenta hushpuppies, and burst tomatoes on serving plates. Sprinkle with the basil and serve.

Makes 12 tacos; serves 4

On a family trip to Hawaii a few years back, my stepbrother Shimon requested fish tacos one night. We had a piece of mahi-mahi that was so fresh that I couldn't bear to fry it, so I opted for pan-cooking it instead. The lighter, cleaner, and super-flavorful result has made the technique my go-to for fish tacos. I keep the slaw and mayo uncomplicated.

Tip I'm a big fan of using a mandoline (or plastic V-slicer) for getting a paper-thin slice on the cabbage for this slaw. The delicate strands not only taste sweeter, they also wilt to become a slaw more quickly when cut that way. Keep your attention as sharp as your blade when using this tool (no texting and driving, please!), and be sure to use the safety guard.

2 large limes

1/4 cup plus 2 tablespoons good-quality mayonnaise, such as Hellmann's, Duke's, or Sir Kensington's

1 teaspoon finely chopped canned chipotle chile in adobo, plus 1 teaspoon of the adobo sauce, or to taste

Kosher salt

3 cups very thinly sliced red cabbage (see Tip)

1 cup coarsely chopped fresh cilantro, plus whole sprigs for garnish

2 tablespoons apple cider vinegar

1/8 teaspoon celery seeds

Freshly ground black pepper

1 tablespoon unsalted butter

1 tablespoon extra-virgin olive oil

1 pound flaky white fish fillets, such as mahi-mahi, cod, hake, or pollack, about 1/2 inch thick

12 (5-inch) white corn tortillas

Optional toppings: Hot sauce, thinly sliced scallions, thinly sliced radishes, and/or pickled jalapeños, store-bought or homemade (page 184)

Grate 1 teaspoon zest from 1 lime, then cut the lime in half. Squeeze 1 tablespoon juice into a small bowl. Set the other lime half aside.

Stir the zest, mayo, chipotle chile, adobo sauce, and ⅛ teaspoon salt into the bowl with the juice. Taste to make sure the sauce has a nice kick but isn't overwhelming, and adjust accordingly.

In a medium bowl, toss together the cabbage, cilantro, vinegar, celery seeds, ½ teaspoon salt, a generous pinch of pepper, and 3 tablespoons of the chipotle mayo to combine well. Cover with plastic wrap, pressing the wrap against the slaw to seal out the air and speed up the marinating process.

continues

In a large nonstick skillet, heat the butter and oil over medium-high heat until the butter melts. Add the fish and cook until the bottom is lightly golden, about 4 minutes. Flip and continue cooking, breaking up the fish into chunks, until it is opaque and beginning to flake, 6 to 8 minutes. Season with ¼ teaspoon salt, then squeeze the reserved lime half over the top. Remove the pan from the heat.

Line a plate or small basket with a cloth napkin or dishcloth. In a large skillet set over medium heat, heat the tortillas in batches, turning occasionally, until they puff and are golden in spots, 2 to 3 minutes. Transfer the warm tortillas to the prepared plate as you go and wrap them in the napkin to keep them warm and pliable. (Alternatively, you can make two stacks of tortillas, wrap them in foil, and warm in a low oven.)

To serve the tacos, cut the remaining lime into wedges. Smear about 1 teaspoon of the chipotle mayo over each tortilla. Place a few nuggets of fish on top. Top the tacos with the slaw and fresh cilantro sprigs. Squeeze the lime wedges over the top. Serve the tacos immediately, passing any of the optional toppings at the table.

Smoky Chicken Skillet Fajitas
(page 184)

Smoky Chicken Skillet Fajitas

Serves 4

My *Queer Eye* castmates Tan and Jonathan would never let me get away without including this recipe, which I'd often cook after a long shoot day together. Charred peppers and onion, zesty lime chicken strips, and quick-pickled jalapeños converge in a fresh, satisfying dish. *The photo is on pages 182–183.*

QUICK-PICKLED JALAPEÑOS

1/4 cup apple cider vinegar

1 1/2 teaspoons sugar

Kosher salt

1 large or 2 medium jalapeño or serrano chiles, cut into 1/4-inch-thick slices

FAJITAS

1 packed tablespoon grated lime zest (from 1 to 2 limes)

1/4 cup plus 2 tablespoons fresh lime juice (from 3 large limes)

1/4 cup plus 3 tablespoons olive oil

2 tablespoons smoked paprika (pimentón)

1 tablespoon chili powder

Kosher salt

1 1/2 pounds boneless, skinless chicken breasts, cut crosswise into 1/2-inch-thick slices

2 large poblano peppers, cut lengthwise into 1/2-inch-thick strips

1 large onion, halved and cut lengthwise into 1/2-inch-thick slices

3 garlic cloves, thinly sliced

8 (6-inch) flour tortillas

Optional toppings: Greek yogurt or sour cream, cubed avocado, crumbled queso fresco or feta cheese, salsa fresca, thinly sliced scallions, and/or chopped fresh cilantro

Lime wedges for serving

For the pickled jalapeños: In a small bowl, whisk together the vinegar, sugar, and a generous pinch of salt. Stir in the jalapeños. Set aside for at least 30 minutes.

For the fajitas: In a large bowl, stir together the lime zest, 1/4 cup of the lime juice, 1/4 cup of the oil, the smoked paprika, chili powder, and 2 teaspoons salt. Add the chicken and stir to coat. If you have time, let the chicken marinate at room temp for 30 minutes or refrigerated for up to 2 hours. Let the chicken come to room temp before cooking, if it's been refrigerated.

Heat 2 tablespoons of the oil in a large heavy skillet over medium-high heat until hot but not smoking. Add the poblanos and onion and cook, stirring frequently, until the vegetables begin to blister and blacken along the edges, 12 to 15 minutes. Stir in the garlic and a pinch of salt and cook for 1 minute. Stir in ¼ cup water and the remaining 2 tablespoons lime juice. Cook until the liquid is mostly evaporated, then transfer to a bowl. Set the skillet aside. Wipe out the skillet.

Meanwhile, line a plate or small basket with a cloth napkin or dishcloth. In a large skillet set over medium heat, heat the tortillas in batches, turning occasionally, until they puff and are golden in spots, 2 to 3 minutes. Transfer the warm tortillas to the prepared plate as you go and wrap them in the napkin to keep them warm and pliable. (Alternatively, you can wrap the tortillas together in foil and warm in a low oven.)

Drain the chicken from the marinade and transfer to a plate. Return the skillet you used for the veg to medium-high heat. Add the remaining tablespoon of oil and heat until hot. Add the chicken and cook, stirring occasionally, until cooked through, 5 to 7 minutes. Return the poblanos and onion to the skillet, add a pinch of salt, and stir to combine everything. Remove from the heat.

Drain the pickled chiles, discarding the brine. Dollop a little yogurt or sour cream, if using, on the tortillas, then top with the fajita mixture, pickled chiles, and any additional toppings you like. Squeeze lime wedges over the top and serve.

A dollop of Greek yogurt takes the subtle heat down a notch. The quick-pickled chiles are easy and fun to make, but if you're pressed for time, you can use canned or jarred.

Chicken Milanese with Baby Tomato Salad

Serves 4

The more I learn about food, the more I see dishes that are repeated across cultures. Take Southern fried chicken, for example. Its Italian counterpart is a thinly pounded boneless cutlet, with fairly similar basic ingredients. It skips the brining and messy cooking process, but you still end up with a nice plate of crispy, juicy meat. I jones for this dish all year long, using a mix of local heirloom tomatoes in the summer and sweet cherry (or grape) or Kumato tomatoes during the cooler months.

1½ teaspoons finely chopped shallot or red onion

1 tablespoon fresh lemon juice

Kosher salt

CHICKEN

3 large eggs

Kosher salt and freshly ground black pepper

1½ cups panko bread crumbs

1 cup finely grated Parmesan, preferably Parmigiano-Reggiano (about 3 ounces)

1½ pounds chicken cutlets or boneless, skinless chicken breasts, butterflied and very gently pounded, if necessary, into ¼-inch-thick cutlets (see Tip)

½ cup neutral oil, such as canola, for frying

SALAD

2 tablespoons extra-virgin olive oil

1 pint (about 2 cups) Sungold, cherry, grape, or Kumato tomatoes, cut into halves or quarters if using Kumatos

2 cups loosely packed baby arugula

¼ loosely packed cup fresh flat-leaf parsley leaves, torn if large

¼ loosely packed cup fresh basil leaves, torn if large

3 tablespoons finely chopped roasted, salted pistachios

Freshly ground black pepper

Lemon wedges for serving

The quickest way to a chicken cutlet is to get them already prepared, but if you want to save a few bucks, you can buy boneless, skinless breasts and butterfly the meat into cutlets yourself. You need a good sharp knife (I also recommend a heavy plastic cutting board that can be washed/sanitized in the dishwasher). Then it's just a matter of placing each chicken breast flat on your board and slowly steadying the breast by putting your hand on top as you slice. Then cut through it horizontally until you can open it up like a book.

In a large bowl, combine the shallot or red onion, lemon juice, and ¼ teaspoon salt. Let stand while you prepare the chicken. (This will soften the bite of the shallot or onion and quickly pickle it.)

For the chicken: Heat the oven to 200°F.

In a large shallow bowl, beat the eggs with 1 teaspoon salt and a generous pinch of pepper. In a second large shallow bowl, mix together the panko and Parm. One by one, dip the cutlets in the egg, letting the excess drip off, then gently press into the panko mixture to coat on all sides, and transfer to a large plate. Set a cooling rack on a baking sheet and place near the stove.

Heat the oil in a large skillet (not nonstick) over medium-high heat until very hot but not smoking. Fry the cutlets in two or three batches, turning once, until golden brown and cooked through, 2 to 3 minutes per side. Drain on the prepared rack and, while they're still hot, season them generously with salt. Then transfer the cutlets to the baking sheet and place in the oven to keep warm while you wrap up the batches.

For the salad: Whisk the oil into the lemon-shallot mixture. Add the tomatoes, arugula, parsley, basil, pistachios, and a generous pinch of cracked pepper to the bowl and gently toss to combine.

Arrange the cutlets on serving plates. Mound handfuls of the salad on top and/or the side. Squeeze the lemon wedges over and serve.

Serves 4

I was inspired to make this dish by my sister, who made a Middle Eastern version of it on repeat one summer, seasoning shreds of warm, juicy rotisserie chicken with fresh lemon juice and Mediterranean spices. We were all pretty damn happy about it. I swapped lime juice for the lemon and fresh cilantro for the parsley for a Latin vibe. Enjoy this for dinner with rice or a salad alongside; stuff it into a pita and tote it to work or school; or bring it to a picnic or potluck, where it can stand on its own as part of a big spread of other meat and vegetable dishes.

---

1 small to medium red onion, finely chopped (about 1 cup)

1/4 cup plus 2 tablespoons fresh lime juice (from 3 large limes)

Kosher salt

1 (2 3/4- to 3-pound) rotisserie chicken, meat removed and shredded, skin and bones discarded (about 5 cups chicken)

1 cup finely chopped fresh cilantro leaves and tender stems

Warm pitas or rice, or your favorite salad, for serving

Lime wedges for serving

In a large bowl, stir together the onion, lime juice, and 1 teaspoon salt. Let stand for 10 to 15 minutes while the salt and acid do their magic to soften the texture and bite of the onion.

Add the chicken and cilantro to the onion mixture. Toss to combine. Adjust the salt to taste.

Serve the chicken with warm pitas or rice, or salad, and lime wedges.

Turkey Meatballs

in Velvety Tomato Sauce

Serves 6

I came up with this recipe when my bestie Reema Sampat was pregnant as a way to satisfy her meatball cravings using a lean protein. The sauce is a spin on a recipe by Marcella Hazan. I like to eat the meatballs and sauce on their own accompanied by a salad, but you can also go the spaghetti route (this will sauce about 1½ pounds of pasta nicely), or serve them with crusty bread.

SAUCE

2 (28-ounce) cans whole tomatoes, preferably San Marzano, with their juices

1 medium onion, peeled and cut in half

6 tablespoons (3/4 stick) unsalted butter

Rind from a hunk of Parmigiano-Reggiano (optional)

4 sprigs fresh basil

Kosher salt

MEATBALLS

1/2 teaspoon fennel seeds

2 pounds dark-meat ground turkey

1 cup finely grated Parmesan, preferably Parmigiano-Reggiano (about 3 ounces)

1 large egg

2 teaspoons honey

1/4 teaspoon red pepper flakes

1 teaspoon kosher salt

3 tablespoons olive oil, plus more as needed

FOR SERVING

Freshly grated Parmesan

Freshly ground black pepper

Fresh basil leaves

For the sauce: In a medium saucepan, combine the tomatoes, with their juices, the onion halves, butter, Parm rind, if using, basil, and 1 teaspoon salt. Bring to a gentle simmer and cook on low heat, stirring occasionally and breaking up the tomatoes with a wooden spoon, until the sauce is flavorful and slightly thickened, 45 to 50 minutes. Adjust the seasoning to taste. (*The sauce can be made up to 1 week ahead and refrigerated; remove the Parm, onion, and basil before storing. Or let cool, transfer to freezer containers, and freeze for up to 3 months.*)

Meanwhile, make the meatballs: Toast the fennel seeds in a small dry skillet over medium-low heat, frequently shaking the pan back and forth, until fragrant, about 2 minutes. Transfer the seeds to a cutting board and cool, then coarsely chop.

In a large bowl, combine the fennel seeds, turkey, cheese, egg, honey, red pepper flakes, and salt and, using dampened hands, gently mix together. Form the mixture into 24 (1½-inch) balls, moistening your hands again as necessary.

Tip If you prefer not to fry the meatballs, you can bake them on a lightly oiled foil-lined baking sheet at 425°F until cooked through, 15 to 18 minutes. Any leftover sauce can be saved for a simple pasta.

In a large skillet, heat the oil over medium-high heat until very hot but not smoking. Add enough of the meatballs to fit in a single layer without crowding and cook, turning occasionally, until golden and just cooked through, 10 to 12 minutes. Transfer to a large plate, wipe out the skillet, and repeat with the remaining meatballs, adding more oil as needed. (*The cooked meatballs can be frozen on a parchment-lined baking sheet, and, once firm, transferred to a zipper-lock bag and frozen for up to 3 months. Thaw overnight in the refrigerator.*)

Remove the Parm rind (if you used it), onion halves, and basil sprigs from the sauce. Add the meatballs and gently simmer for 2 to 3 minutes, or until warmed through.

Spoon the meatballs and sauce onto serving plates. Top with Parm, pepper, and basil. Serve hot.

Turkey Kefte

with Hummus + Spicy Crushed Cucumber Salad

Serves 4

Kefte are savory Middle Eastern meat patties, cooked on skewers. I pair them with a crunchy, spicy cucumber salad and homemade hummus. The trio makes for an impressive weeknight staple, and leftovers are perfect for noshing on the following day. I love the extra-creamy consistency of homemade hummus, but in a pinch you can use store-bought and make it nicer by swirling the spread onto a plate, drizzling it with some good olive oil, and sprinkling with several pinches of the spices suggested below.

SPICY CRUSHED CUCUMBER SALAD

3 tablespoons extra-virgin olive oil, plus more for the pan

1 tablespoon chili garlic sauce, sambal oelek, or Sriracha

1 teaspoon honey

Kosher salt

About 2 pounds thin-skinned cucumbers, such as Persian or English (about 12 Persian cukes or 2 large English cukes)

1/3 cup loosely packed fresh mint leaves, torn if large

KEFTE

1 1/2 pounds dark-meat ground turkey

1 small onion, finely chopped (about 3/4 cup)

2 tablespoons finely chopped fresh mint

2 teaspoons kosher salt

1 1/2 teaspoons ground cumin

1 teaspoon red pepper flakes

1/2 teaspoon ground cinnamon

1/4 teaspoon freshly ground black pepper

HUMMUS

2 (15.5-ounce) cans chickpeas, rinsed and drained

1/4 cup plus 2 tablespoons well-stirred tahini

1/4 cup fresh lemon juice (from 1 1/2 to 2 large lemons)

1 garlic clove, very thinly sliced

1 1/2 teaspoons kosher salt

Extra-virgin olive oil for drizzling

A few pinches of of za'atar or ground cumin and/or smoked paprika (pimentón) for garnish (optional)

continues

For the cucumber salad: In a large bowl, whisk together the oil, chili garlic sauce, honey, and ¼ teaspoon salt. Set aside.

Cut larger cukes lengthwise in half. Trim the ends of whichever cukes you are using and cut into 2-inch lengths. Place the pieces in a large zipper-lock bag and seal the bag. Give the bag a few whacks with a small skillet or rolling pin until the cuke pieces split apart. Transfer the cucumbers to a colander set over a bowl and toss with 1½ teaspoons salt. Let drain, tossing once or twice, while you prepare the kefte and hummus (at least 20 minutes).

I use the oven to bake these kefte, so that I am free to make my salad and hummus while they cook, but you can shape the kefte onto flat skewers and grill them indoors on a grill pan or outside on a gas or charcoal grill.

For the kefte: Heat the oven to 425°F, with a rack in the lower third. Line a baking sheet with foil and lightly grease with oil.

In a large bowl, combine the turkey, onion, mint, salt, cumin, red pepper flakes, cinnamon, and black pepper and, using dampened hands, gently mix together. Divide the mixture into 8 portions and form into torpedo-shaped patties, each about 4 inches long. Arrange on the baking sheet. Bake the kefte, rotating the baking sheet and turning the patties once halfway through, until golden and cooked through, 20 to 22 minutes. Transfer to a platter.

Meanwhile, make the hummus: Set aside ¼ cup of the chickpeas for garnish. Pulse the remaining chickpeas with the tahini, lemon juice, garlic, salt, and ½ cup ice water in a food processor until smooth, adding more ice water by the tablespoon to thin to the desired consistency if necessary. *(The hummus can be made up to 3 days ahead, covered, and refrigerated.)*

Spread the hummus on a serving plate. Swirl with a spatula. Drizzle with oil, then top with the reserved chickpeas and sprinkle with the spices, if using.

Transfer the cucumbers to the bowl with the chili garlic sauce mixture. Add about ¼ cup of the mint and toss to combine. Top with the remaining mint leaves. Serve with the kefte and hummus.

Serves 4 to 6

Moroccan-Style Pasta Bolognese

Cumin, coriander, and cinnamon—as well as lamb rather than the traditional beef—give this classic meat sauce a little spin. Since the sauce makes enough for 2 pounds of pasta, I make it on a lazy Sunday and freeze half of it (or all of it, in two batches) for a no-fuss weeknight meal or weekend dinner later on.

Kosher salt

1 pound long pasta, such as tagliatelle, fettuccine, linguine, or spaghetti

¾ cup full-fat plain Greek yogurt

1 tablespoon unsalted butter

2½ cups Moroccan Lamb Bolognese Sauce (page 196), warmed

Coarsely chopped fresh cilantro or mint

Freshly grated Parmigiano-Reggiano for serving

Freshly ground black pepper

Bring a large pot of water to a boil and salt 'til it tastes like the ocean (taste it). Add the pasta and cook, stirring, until al dente.

Meanwhile, in a small bowl, stir together the yogurt and 1 to 2 tablespoons of the pasta cooking liquid to loosen it just a bit. Set aside.

Scoop out about ¾ cup of the pasta cooking liquid and reserve. Drain the pasta and return it to the pot. Add the butter, Bolognese sauce, and a tablespoon or two of the pasta cooking liquid. Toss together to combine, adding more pasta cooking liquid by the tablespoonful if the pasta appears dry.

Transfer to serving bowls. Dollop with the yogurt and top with cilantro or mint, Parm, and black pepper.

continues

Moroccan Lamb Bolognese Sauce

Makes 5 cups

2 tablespoons extra-virgin olive oil

2 tablespoons unsalted butter

1/2 small onion, finely chopped (about 3/4 cup)

2 medium carrots, finely chopped

2 celery stalks, finely chopped

2 garlic cloves, finely chopped

1 1/2 pounds ground lamb

1 3/4 teaspoons ground cumin

1 1/4 teaspoons ground coriander

3/4 teaspoon red pepper flakes

1/2 teaspoon ground cinnamon

Kosher salt and freshly ground black pepper

3/4 cup whole milk

3/4 cup dry red wine

1 (28-ounce) can whole tomatoes, preferably San Marzano, with their juices

In a large Dutch oven or other wide heavy pot, heat the oil and butter over medium heat until the butter is melted and foamy. Add the onion, carrots, celery, and garlic and cook, stirring occasionally, until the onion is softened and translucent, 6 to 8 minutes. Add the lamb and cook, stirring frequently and breaking up the meat into bits with a wooden spoon, until cooked through, about 6 minutes.

Stir in the cumin, coriander, red pepper flakes, cinnamon, ¾ teaspoon salt, and a generous pinch of pepper and cook for 30 seconds. Stir in the milk. Bring to a simmer, then reduce the heat to medium-low and gently simmer until the sauce is thickened, 3 to 5 minutes. Add the wine and simmer until mostly evaporated, 8 to 10 minutes more.

Add the tomatoes and their juices, then reduce the heat to low. Break up the tomatoes into smaller pieces with a wooden spoon, then gently simmer, uncovered, stirring occasionally and adding water by ½ cupfuls if the sauce becomes dry, until the sauce is deeply flavorful, about 3 hours. Remove from the heat and adjust the seasoning to taste. Serve, or let cool before storing. (*The sauce can be refrigerated for up to 3 days or frozen for up to 3 months. Thaw if frozen and gently reheat over low heat, stirring occasionally, and adding 2 to 4 tablespoons water as necessary before serving.*)

For quick work, you can chop the onion, carrot, celery, and garlic together in a food processor.

Szynka VIRGINIA 6 99 Lb
Szynka BLACK FOREST 6 99 Lb
Pieczeń RZYMSK 5 39 Lb
Pasztet 5 39 Lb
Gotowana Wędzo

Kielbasa Polish-Style

Serves 4

Traditional Polish kielbasa is sweet, garlicky, and smoky, best enjoyed crisped up on a grill or in a skillet, accompanied by sauerkraut or braised cabbage and boiled potatoes. It's the hot dog's brawny older Eastern European uncle. Serve it solo, or proudly serve to a crowd on a charcuterie board; or, for easy outdoor entertaining, serve with a good pale lager-style beer.

1½ teaspoons olive oil

1½ pounds kielbasa (ideally from a Polish market), cut in half lengthwise and scored on the skin side

FOR SERVING

Finely chopped fresh flat-leaf parsley or dill

Sauerkraut, at room temp

Hot mustard, ideally Polish

Heat the oil in a large skillet over medium-high heat. Add the kielbasa, cut side down, and cook, turning occasionally, until deeply golden, about 4 minutes.

Serve hot, topped with parsley or dill, with sauerkraut and mustard alongside.

My favorite Polish extra-hot mustard is Cracovia Dobra Tesciowa (*dobra tesciowa* means "good mother-in-law"). When I can't find it outside New York or Montreal, I make an ad hoc version by stirring a squirt or two of Sriracha and a touch of honey into some hot Dijon.

Serves 4

Hanger steak is relatively lean but packed with flavor. Lime juice and a heap of mint and cilantro leaves make the dish salady and satisfying, and give it an Asian twist.

2 large limes, cut in half

1 large shallot, thinly sliced (about ⅓ cup)

Kosher salt

2 large garlic cloves, grated or finely chopped

1 tablespoon packed grated peeled fresh ginger

3½ tablespoons olive oil, plus more for brushing and grilling

1½ to 2 pounds hanger steak, about 1 inch thick, center line of gristle removed

Freshly ground black pepper

¼ cup loosely packed mixed fresh basil, mint, and/or cilantro leaves

1 jalapeño, thinly sliced

Squeeze 2 teaspoons juice from one of the lime halves. Put the juice in a bowl and stir in the shallot and ¼ teaspoon salt. Set aside.

In a large bowl, mix together the garlic, ginger, and 1 tablespoon of the oil. Add the steak and turn to coat. Let stand for 10 minutes.

Heat a lightly oiled gas or charcoal grill to high or heat in an oiled grill pan over high heat. (On a charcoal grill, most of the coals should be covered with white ash, and you should be able to hold your palm an inch or two above the cooking grate for no more than 2 to 3 seconds.)

Brush the cut sides of the remaining lime halves with a total of 1½ teaspoons oil and season with a generous pinch each of salt and pepper.

Scrape the marinade from the steak and season with 1¼ teaspoons salt and ½ teaspoon pepper. Grill the steak, turning once, until nicely charred, 4 to 5 minutes per side. (Go for 130°F if you're using an instant-read thermometer to check doneness.) At the same time, grill the lime halves, cut side down, rotating them occasionally, until charred, about 5 minutes. Transfer the limes and steak to a cutting board and let rest for 15 minutes.

Stir the remaining 2 tablespoons oil into the shallot mixture.

Slice the steak crosswise into ½-inch-thick pieces and arrange on a platter. Squeeze the grilled lime wedges over, then spoon the shallot vinaigrette on top. Top with the herbs and chile.

Hanger steak has a line of gristle that runs down the middle. You can ask your butcher to remove it or do it at home before marinating. If you can't get hanger, skirt steak is also good here; cook it for slightly less time, 3 to 4 minutes per side.

ANIMAL

Serves 4

Roasting a whole fish is great for a dinner party or a date night in because it's impressive and mostly hands-off. The fishmonger cleans and scales the fish, then you get to stuff it with aromatics like citrus and fresh herbs, which impart their delicate flavors as it roasts. While you have the oven on, you can throw in an easy side, like Roasted Potato Wedges with Montreal Steak Seasoning (page 105) or Asparagus with Oozy Eggs (page 88). Oh, and please don't forget to go for the cheek meat from the head of the fish—it's sweet and really the very best part. *The photo is on pages 206–207.*

---

1 (2½- to 3-pound) red snapper, cleaned and scaled, head and tail left intact

Kosher salt and freshly ground black pepper

1 lemon, thinly sliced into rounds, seeds removed

6 fresh flat-leaf parsley sprigs, plus chopped fresh parsley for serving

3 bay leaves

½ teaspoon dried oregano

2 small red onions, cut into ½-inch wedges, leaving some of the stem end intact

¼ cup plus 2 tablespoons dry white wine

⅓ cup extra-virgin olive oil

Heat the oven to 450°F, with a rack in the middle.

Rinse the fish and pat dry. Cut 3 crosswise slashes down to the bone on each side of the fish. Season the cavity and skin generously with salt and pepper. Stuff the slashes on the top side of the fish with a few lemon slices, then stuff the cavity with the parsley sprigs, bay leaves, oregano, and remaining lemon slices.

In a roasting pan that's large enough to accommodate the fish, toss the onion wedges with ½ teaspoon salt and ¼ teaspoon pepper, then drizzle with the wine and about half of the oil. Arrange the onion wedges in a single layer to form a bed for the fish. Place the fish on top and drizzle with the remaining oil.

Roast until the fish is cooked through, 25 to 30 minutes. To check for doneness, use the tip of a paring knife to pull back a bit of the meat in the thickest part of the fish. If the meat is opaque down to the bone, you're good to go.

Any whole fish can be roasted in this manner. If snapper isn't available, try sea bass, blackfish, sea bream, branzino, or Arctic char. If the fish are smaller than what is called for in this recipe, roast two or more to feed the same amount of eaters. Remember to adjust the cooking time, as smaller fish will cook faster.

Transfer the fish and onions to a serving platter. Drizzle with the pan juices and top with the chopped parsley.

To serve, run the tip of a paring knife down the backbone of the fish, then do the same along the collarbone (right behind the head) and at the tail end of the fish. Cut the top fillet in half without cutting through the bone, slip a small metal spatula under it, and gently push, lift, and transfer each one to a serving plate. Starting at the tail end, lift off the backbone. Remove any visible bones from the bottom fillet, halve, and transfer each piece to the serving plate. Serve with the onions, drizzled with any remaining pan juices.

Whole Roasted Red Snapper with Lemon and Herbs *(page 204)*

WITH CARROT BUTTER + CRISPY CAPERS

Serves 4

These scallops get a simple sauce of butter, carrot juice, and citrus, with crispy capers on top. Frying the little buds in olive oil is a trick I owe to my good pal and old boss, the famed Canadian chef Chuck Hughes.

CRISPY CAPERS

Olive oil for shallow-frying

3 tablespoons capers, drained and patted dry

SCALLOPS

4 tablespoons (1/2 stick) unsalted butter

1¼ cups fresh carrot juice

2 tablespoons fresh orange juice

Kosher salt and freshly ground black pepper

1 pound dry sea scallops, rinsed, tough muscles removed, and patted dry

Finely chopped fresh flat-leaf parsley or tarragon for garnish

For the capers: Line a plate with paper towels. Pour ½ inch of oil into a small skillet and heat over medium-high heat until very hot and shimmering but not smoking. Carefully add the capers (the oil will splatter a bit) and fry until the edges are puffed up and lightly golden, 30 to 60 seconds. Using a slotted spoon, transfer the capers to the paper towels to drain.

For the scallops: Cut 2 tablespoons of the butter into cubes and return to the refrigerator. In a small saucepan, bring the carrot juice to a low boil over medium-high heat and cook until reduced by half, 10 to 12 minutes. Reduce to a simmer, then whisk in the chilled butter one cube at a time, whisking constantly and allowing each cube to completely blend in with the sauce before adding the next. Whisk in the orange juice, ¼ teaspoon salt, and a generous pinch of pepper. Remove from the heat.

Lightly season the scallops with salt on both sides. In a large nonstick skillet, heat the remaining 2 tablespoons butter over medium-high heat until melted and foaming. Add the scallops and cook, tipping the pan to the side so the butter pools and basting the scallops with the butter, until a golden crust forms along the lower edges of each one, 2 to 3 minutes. Flip and continue cooking until the scallops are just cooked through, 30 seconds to 1 minute more. (They should be golden brown on their tops and bottoms but still a bit undercooked and somewhat creamy in the very center.)

Transfer the scallops to serving plates, drizzle with the carrot butter, and garnish with the crispy capers and chopped herbs.

Tip Look for scallops labeled "dry," also called diver scallops. "Wet" scallops (usually not labeled as such) are preserved in a solution of water and chemicals, which dilutes their natural flavor and makes them heavier (and therefore more expensive). And it leaches out during cooking, steaming them, so they don't sear. Most scallops have a tough little muscle attached. Pull off and discard before cooking.

Pineapple and Shrimp Skewers with Green Sauce

Serves 4

Here's a great, easy party dish. You've got a little fruit and sweetness from the pineapple, a spicy kick from the ginger and chiles, and a hint of funk from the fish sauce. You can assemble the skewers ahead and grill them whenever you're ready. Since they are as good warm as they are at room temp, they can be noshed on over several hours. If you're lucky enough to have leftovers, slide the ingredients off the skewers and toss with your favorite lettuces for an awesome salad. The green sauce is your dressing, built right in.

SKEWERS

1 pound large shrimp, peeled and deveined

2 cups ½-inch chunks fresh pineapple

1 medium red onion, cut into ½-inch-thick wedges, leaving some of the stem end intact

GREEN SAUCE

2 tablespoons grated lime zest (from about 2 large limes)

¼ cup plus 2 tablespoons fresh lime juice (from about 3 large limes)

2 tablespoons fish sauce

2 tablespoons finely chopped fresh cilantro leaves and tender stems

1 tablespoon packed brown sugar

½ teaspoon grated peeled fresh ginger

1 tablespoon extra-virgin olive oil, plus more for the grill

Thinly sliced fresh Thai bird, Fresno, or serrano chiles and chopped fresh cilantro for serving

Since the shrimp cook more quickly than the onion and pineapple, it's best to grill them separately.

For the skewers: Choose 12 skewers. If using wooden ones, soak them in water for 10 minutes. Thread the shrimp onto skewers. Thread the pineapple and onion onto the skewers, alternating them as you go.

Heat a lightly oiled gas or charcoal grill to medium-high or an oiled grill pan over medium-high heat. (On a charcoal grill, most of the coals should be covered with white ash, and you should be able to hold your palm an inch or two over the cooking grate for no more than 2 to 3 seconds.)

Grill the skewers, turning once, until the shrimp are opaque and cooked through and the pineapple is charred, about 2 minutes per side for the shrimp, and 4 minutes per side for the pineapple/onion. Remove from the grill.

For the green sauce: In a blender, combine all of the ingredients *except* the oil and pulse. With the machine running, slowly add the oil to combine.

Arrange the skewers on a platter and drizzle with about ¼ cup of the sauce. Top with fresh chiles and cilantro. Serve warm or at room temperature, with the remaining sauce on the side.

Alaskan King Crab Legs

with Tarragon-Lemon Butter

Serves 2

Alaskan king crab is probably as decadent as it gets with seafood, and you don't need to do much for it to be awesomely delicious. I serve it when I need to make amends to someone, or when I just got paid and am feeling flush. It's certainly not for every day unless you're a sheik or an oligarch, but it's perfect for any special occasion.

---

8 tablespoons (1 stick) salted or cultured butter

1 teaspoon grated lemon zest

1 teaspoon fresh lemon juice

1½ teaspoons packed fresh tarragon leaves, torn if large

3 to 4 pounds frozen cooked Alaskan king crab legs, thawed

In a medium saucepan, melt the butter over medium heat. Whisk in the lemon zest and juice until fully incorporated, then stir in the tarragon. Remove from the heat and cover to keep warm.

Fill a wide shallow serving bowl with crushed ice. Arrange the crab legs on top. Serve with the warm butter for dipping, and plenty of paper towels.

HOW TO EAT KING CRAB LEGS: Start by breaking apart the legs at their natural hinges, removing any stiff pieces of cartilage. Use your fingers or a lobster pick to pull out the meat from the cavities. Using the tip of a sharp paring knife, and working along the lightest-colored side of the shells (these are the thinnest and most easily breakable parts), split the shells lengthwise. With your fingers, snap them open to get at the meat inside. If you have claws, use a lobster cracker.

劉氏
藥房
218 WIN SEA FOOD MARKET
NEW YORK LOTTERY

Malaysian Chili Shrimp

Serves 4

I discovered Malaysian cooking as a short-lived lunch waiter at Zak Pelaccio's Fatty Crab in New York City. I'd roll in, usually hungover from a raucous night, and head straight to the kitchen for a bowl of rice, which I'd top with a spoonful of crab in chili sauce and a heap of chopped cilantro. Fatty Crab has since closed, but this spin-off of one of Zak's most famous recipes keeps the love alive.

1½ cups jasmine or other long-grain white rice

3 tablespoons low-sodium soy sauce

3 tablespoons tomato paste

2 tablespoons chili garlic sauce or sambal oelek

1 tablespoon plus 1 teaspoon sugar

1 tablespoon toasted sesame oil

1 tablespoon extra-virgin olive oil

½ cup finely chopped red onion

2 garlic cloves, finely chopped

1 tablespoon grated peeled fresh ginger

1½ pounds jumbo shrimp, peeled and deveined

2 scallions, thinly sliced

½ cup coarsely chopped fresh cilantro

Cook the rice according to the instructions on the package.

Meanwhile, whisk together the soy sauce, tomato paste, chili garlic sauce, sugar, sesame oil, and 1 cup water in a bowl.

In a very large skillet, heat the olive oil over medium heat until very hot but not smoking. Add the onion, garlic, and ginger and cook, stirring frequently, until tender and lightly golden, 5 to 7 minutes (reduce the heat if the mixture is browning too quickly). Add the soy sauce mixture, bring to a gentle simmer, and cook for 4 minutes, whisking occasionally, to slightly thicken the sauce and let the flavors blend.

Nestle the shrimp into the sauce. Gently simmer, turning the shrimp once halfway through, until opaque and just cooked through, 4 to 5 minutes (or less for smaller shrimp; see Tip). Using a slotted spoon, transfer the shrimp to a bowl. Continue to simmer the sauce, whisking occasionally, for 1 to 2 minutes more to slightly thicken. Remove the pan from the heat.

Spoon the rice onto serving plates. Spoon the shrimp on top. Top with the sauce, scallions, and cilantro, and serve.

Tip

I love meaty jumbo shrimp for this recipe; there are generally 16 to 20 shrimp per pound (labeled "16/20"). Since the names for shrimp sizes are unregulated (one shop's "jumbo" is another one's "extra large"), it's best to look at the numbers. If the big guys are not available, you can use smaller ones; just keep an eye on your cook time (smaller shrimp will cook more quickly). If using smaller shrimp, when they are done, use a slotted spoon to remove them from the sauce and let the sauce simmer for 2 to 3 more minutes to thicken slightly.

Chile-Maple Roasted Chicken

Serves 4

A roast chicken is a blank slate. Once you have the technique down, you can apply any flavors you like. This recipe came about when I lived in Brooklyn and was studying acting, and cooking for my roommates, PJ and Ben, also fledgling creatives. Using the only spices we had in the larder, plus the insanely good maple syrup my father sends me from Vermont, I made this ad hoc and utterly delicious dish. It's now my numero uno.

---

4 tablespoons (½ stick) unsalted butter, at room temperature

2 tablespoons pure maple syrup

2 teaspoons chili powder

2 teaspoons ground dried chipotle chile or ¼ teaspoon cayenne pepper

1 (4½- to 5-pound) chicken

Kosher salt

½ lemon

½ small onion, unpeeled, cut into wedges

5 garlic cloves, gently smashed but not peeled

Freshly ground black pepper

Heat the oven to 425°F, with a rack in the middle.

In a small bowl, stir together the butter, maple syrup, chili powder, and chipotle powder or cayenne until smooth.

Pull off and discard any excess fat around the cavity and neck of the chicken, then pat the chicken thoroughly dry, inside and out. Season the cavity with salt. Squeeze the lemon juice into the cavity and toss in the lemon half, along with the onion and garlic. Starting from the edge of the cavity, slip a finger under the skin of each breast and loosen the skin from the meat of both the breasts and thighs, then spread half of the maple butter mixture under the skin. Rub the remaining butter on top of the skin, then season with 2 teaspoons salt and a generous pinch of pepper.

Place the bird breast side up in a roasting pan or 9-x-13-inch baking dish and roast for 15 minutes. Reduce the heat to 350°F and continue roasting, basting occasionally with the juices, until the juices run clear when the thigh is pierced with a fork, or an instant-read thermometer inserted into the thickest part of the thigh reads 165°F, 65 to 75 minutes more. Remove the bird from the oven and let rest in the pan for 15 minutes.

Baste the chicken with the juices. Transfer to a cutting board and let rest for 5 minutes more, then carve and serve.

Souvlaki Arahova

Serves 4

I'm told that when my mother was pregnant with yours truly, she craved the souvlaki at Arahova in Montreal, our family's favorite Mediterranean place. So I guess I can honestly say that my lifelong love affair with Greek food began in the womb. While I no longer get to eat weekly at Arahova, I now make my own version of their souvlaki—grilled chicken topped with a creamy yogurt and cucumber sauce. I think mine's just as good as the one I remember.

---

2 medium cucumbers, cut into ¼-inch cubes

Kosher salt

1 large garlic clove, coarsely chopped

1 (17.6-ounce) container full-fat plain Greek yogurt

¼ cup fresh lemon juice (from 1 to 2 large lemons)

¼ cup finely chopped fresh dill, plus more for garnish

1¼ to 1½ pounds boneless, skinless chicken breasts, cut into 1½-inch cubes

1 medium shallot, thinly sliced lengthwise

3 tablespoons red wine vinegar

1 cup crumbled feta cheese (about 4 ounces)

1 teaspoon dried oregano

1½ tablespoons extra-virgin olive oil

4 (7- to 8-inch) pocketless pita breads

Freshly ground black pepper

8 ounces Kumato, Campari, or cherry tomatoes, chopped

¼ cup loosely packed fresh mint leaves

Set a colander over a plate. Add the cucumbers, toss with ¼ teaspoon salt, and let stand for 15 minutes.

Mound the garlic and ¼ teaspoon salt on a cutting board. Using a chef's knife, mash and chop into a paste. Transfer to a medium bowl. Stir in the yogurt, lemon juice, and dill.

Transfer about half of the yogurt mixture to a second medium bowl. Stir in the chicken. Cover and refrigerate for at least 45 minutes, or up to 4 hours.

continues

Squeeze the cucumbers to release the liquid. Discard the liquid and stir the cucumber into the remaining yogurt mixture—which is now tzatziki. Cover and refrigerate.

When ready to serve, heat the oven to 200°F. Choose 12 skewers. If using wooden ones, soak them in water for 10 minutes. Remove the tzatziki from the fridge and let it stand at room temp to take the chill off.

Place the shallot in a small bowl and stir in the vinegar and ¼ teaspoon salt. Set aside for 15 minutes to pickle, then drain.

In another small bowl, stir together the feta, oregano, and olive oil.

Heat a lightly oiled gas or charcoal grill to medium-high, or heat an oiled grill pan over medium-high heat. (On a charcoal grill, the coals should be covered with white ash and you should be able to hold your palm an inch or two above the cooking grate for no more than 2 to 3 seconds.)

Meanwhile, warm the pitas in the oven, directly on the racks.

Thread the chicken onto the skewers, then season generously with salt and pepper; discard the marinade. Grill the chicken, turning once halfway through, until cooked through, 8 to 10 minutes. Slide off the skewers and onto a plate.

To serve, put the pitas on serving plates. Spread a dollop of tzatziki onto each pita. Top with the chicken, feta, tomatoes, pickled shallots, a few dollops more of tzatziki, and the mint and chopped dill.

Chicken Livers in Chili Garlic Sauce

WITH BLACKENED ONIONS

Serves 4

As we stepped onto the tarmac at London Heathrow upon arriving in England on a press tour for *Queer Eye*, Tan said, "We *have* to go to Nandos immediately." Since he typically opts for sweets, I was surprised at his enthusiasm for this hometown fast-food joint, but I soon understood why. The chicken livers in chili sauce resuscitated my love for the rich, delicious organ meat. My version adds blackened onions, an ingredient typically used in a Polish variation on this dish.

1¼ pounds chicken livers, cut in half

Kosher salt and freshly ground black pepper

½ cup chili garlic sauce or sambal oelek, plus more for dipping

2 tablespoons fresh lemon juice

3 tablespoons olive oil

2 medium red onions (about 1½ pounds), cut into ¼-inch-thick slices

2 tablespoons unsalted butter

¼ cup finely chopped fresh flat-leaf parsley

Pat the chicken livers dry with paper towels. Season with ¼ teaspoon salt and ⅛ teaspoon pepper.

In a small bowl, stir together the chili garlic sauce (or sambal oelek) and lemon juice; set aside.

In a very large cast-iron skillet, heat 2 tablespoons of the oil over medium-high heat until hot. Add the onions, ½ teaspoon salt, and a generous pinch of black pepper and cook, stirring frequently, until the onions are deeply golden and blackened in spots, 15 to 20 minutes.

Move the onions to the perimeter of the skillet. Add the butter and the remaining tablespoon oil to the center of the pan and heat until the butter melts. Fry the chicken livers, turning once, until browned on the outside, with a little char, but still pink in the center, about 2 minutes per side. Stir in the reserved chili garlic sauce mixture and cook until the sauce thickens a bit, about 2 minutes more.

Remove from the heat and gently stir in the parsley. Serve hot.

Tip Nandos uses bottled peri-peri (aka piri-piri) sauce, which is not widely available in American supermarkets. A combo of chili garlic sauce or sambal oelek and lemon juice runs a close second, or you can purchase bottled peri-peri at gourmet shops or online.

Serves 6 to 8

Turkey Meatloaf with a Block of Sharp Cheddar

My dear former boyfriend Joey and I had a tradition of cooking Sunday dinner for his parents. My deep appreciation for their taking me in as one of their own was reciprocated in the best way I knew to convey it: with a meatloaf stuffed with an entire block of my very favorite cheddar ever, from Cabot Creamery in Vermont. Nothing brings me more joy than cheese oozing out of what is essentially a very tasty giant meatball.

Cold leftovers the next day = SO good. A nice thick slice with a bit of mayo and some butter lettuce makes a fantastic sandwich.

---

1 large onion, coarsely chopped

2 large garlic cloves

2 tablespoons olive oil

Kosher salt

1 cup finely chopped fresh flat-leaf parsley leaves and tender stems

2 teaspoons Worcestershire sauce

2 teaspoons grated lemon zest

1½ teaspoons ground coriander

½ teaspoon red pepper flakes

⅓ cup plus ¼ cup ketchup

1¼ cups panko bread crumbs

½ cup whole milk

2 large eggs, lightly beaten

2 pounds ground turkey, 85% or 93% lean (a mix of light and dark meat)

1 (8-ounce) block sharp cheddar cheese, at room temperature

1 tablespoon packed light or dark brown sugar

1 teaspoon freshly ground black pepper

Heat the oven to 400°F, with a rack in the middle.

Pulse the onion and garlic in a food processor until finely chopped.

Heat the oil in a large skillet over medium-high heat. Add the onion mixture and 1 teaspoon salt and cook, stirring occasionally, until the onion is well softened, about 7 minutes. Remove from the heat. Stir in the parsley, Worcestershire sauce, lemon zest, coriander, red pepper flakes, and ¼ cup of the ketchup, transfer to a large bowl, and let cool.

In a large bowl, stir together the panko and milk and let soak for 5 minutes.

Stir the eggs into the milk mixture, then add to the onion mixture. Add the turkey and ½ teaspoon salt and mix well with your hands.

Lightly oil a 13-x-9-inch baking pan. Shape about half of the meat mixture into a 9-x-5-inch rectangle in the center of the pan. Gently press the cheese into the center, then cover with the remaining meat, building a little wall (about 1½ inches thick) along the sides of the cheese block and on top, being sure to seal all the seams.

Mix together the brown sugar, black pepper, and the remaining ⅓ cup ketchup, then brush on top of the loaf. Bake until the top is deeply golden and the bottom edges are crisp, 50 to 60 minutes. Remove the meatloaf from the oven and let stand for 10 to 15 minutes before serving.

Cast-Iron Butter-Basted Steak

Serves 4

Recently I met a guy about to start college who'd never prepared a meal for himself. He loved steak but didn't have access to a barbecue, so I decided to teach him the technique of butter-basting in a cast-iron skillet. Butter-basting bathes the meat with herbs and salt-flavored fat as it cooks, helping the outside crisp while the inside stays juicy and moist.

---

2 (1- to 1¼-pound) sirloin, boneless rib-eye, or New York strip steaks, 1¼ to 1½ inches thick

1½ teaspoons kosher salt

2 teaspoons neutral oil, such as canola

2 tablespoons unsalted butter

3 leafy sprigs fresh thyme

1 leafy sprig fresh rosemary

2 garlic cloves, gently smashed but not peeled

Coarsely ground black pepper

Pat the steaks dry with paper towels, then season on both sides with the salt, pressing the seasoning into the meat so that it sticks.

Heat a large cast-iron skillet over medium-high heat until very hot. (Give your pan 1 to 2 minutes to heat up; this will help you get a nice dark crust.) Meanwhile, blot the steaks with paper towels on both sides to absorb excess moisture.

Add the oil to the skillet and swirl the pan to coat. Add the steaks and cook, undisturbed, until the undersides are deeply golden and a crust has formed, about 5 minutes. Turn and cook until the second side is deeply golden, about 4 minutes more. Sear the edges of the steaks if they have fat on them, then lay them flat in the pan. Add the butter, thyme, rosemary, garlic, and a generous pinch of pepper to the skillet, then tilt the skillet so that the butter pools to one side and, using a large spoon, baste the steaks with the butter, herbs, and garlic for 1 minute (at this point, an instant-read thermometer inserted into the thickest part should register 120° to 125°F for medium-rare). Remove from the heat.

Transfer the steaks to a cutting board, leaving the juices in the pan. Let rest for 10 minutes.

Cut the steak against the grain into thick slices and arrange on plates. Spoon the pan juices and any collected resting juices over the steak and serve.

Serves 4

There's a magical little taverna on the island of Mykonos, near Agios Sostis Beach, that's run single-handedly by a gentleman named Vassily. To get there, you park your doorless Jimny rental 4x4 and walk a half-mile down a skinny shrub-lined path until you reach a little break in the hillside, and there is Kiki's Taverna. For a meal here, you leave your name, since no reservations are accepted. And while you wait at least an hour for a table, you sip on Greek rosé from copper cups and watch the stray cats roam over the shack-like restaurant's roof. Once you're finally seated, order all of the five salads, and the Kiki's Taverna pork chop. This is not just a pork chop. It is THE pork chop. Glazed in honey and speckled with fresh oregano, it is hands down the juiciest, most delicious piece of pork you will ever eat. With porky juices dribbling down your chin and a stupid smile on your face, you can gaze at the mega-yachts floating in the water in the cove down below and think, "This is the life."

Until you're able to get there, make this dish, which is not the official Kiki's chop but one inspired by my memory of it. *The photo is on page 227.*

---

4 (8- to 10-ounce) bone-in pork rib chops, 1½ inches thick

3 lemons

¼ cup honey

3 tablespoons finely chopped fresh oregano

4 garlic cloves, thinly sliced

2 tablespoons extra-virgin olive oil

Kosher salt

Freshly ground black pepper

Score the fat along the edges of the pork chops (this helps them stay flat as they cook) and place in a zipper-lock bag. Thinly slice 2 of the lemons into rounds. Remove and discard the seeds. Add the slices to the bag with the pork chops.

Continues

In a small bowl, whisk together the honey, oregano, garlic, 1 tablespoon of the oil, ½ teaspoon salt, and 2 tablespoons lukewarm water and pour onto the chops. Press the air out of the bag, then tightly seal. Rub the outside of the bag to mix the marinade, squishing it around the chops to coat. Marinate in the refrigerator for at least 4 hours, or as long as overnight.

Heat the oven to 425°F, with a rack in the middle. Let the chops stand at room temperature (still in the marinade) for 20 minutes to take the chill off.

Remove the pork chops from the marinade, scraping off any lemon or garlic pieces; discard the marinade. Season on all sides with 1 teaspoon salt.

Heat a large ovenproof skillet over medium-high heat until hot. Add the remaining tablespoon of oil to the skillet, then add the chops. Cook until the bottoms are golden, about 5 minutes. Stand the chops on their fatty sides and brown the fat, about 3 minutes, then turn the chops uncooked side down.

Place the pan in the oven and cook until the internal temperature of the chops reads 135°F on an instant-read thermometer, 7 to 9 minutes. Transfer the chops to a large plate and let rest for 5 to 10 minutes.

Meanwhile, cut the remaining lemon into wedges.

Sprinkle the pork chops with a generous pinch or two of pepper and salt. Serve with the lemon wedges.

Pork Chop like at Kiki's Taverna and Braised Red Cabbage with Pears and Cumin *(page 92)*

Serves 4

Rosemary Pork Tenderloin

with Maple-Bourbon Onion Jam

Polish people love pork tenderloin; it's our filet mignon. Searing this lean cut in butter and oil before finishing it in the oven, as opposed to simply roasting it, allows a nice crust to build. I grew up eating this with peaches or apples that were often cooked into a compote. Here a sweet onion jam, spiked with a little booze, makes a good stand-in.

MAPLE-BOURBON ONION JAM

2 tablespoons unsalted butter

1 tablespoon olive oil

1½ pounds red onions, cut into ¼-inch pieces (about 4½ cups)

Kosher salt

⅓ cup pure maple syrup

¼ cup bourbon

½ teaspoon freshly ground black pepper

ROSEMARY PORK TENDERLOIN

4 large garlic cloves, thinly sliced

Kosher salt

2 tablespoons grainy Dijon mustard

1 tablespoon plus 1 teaspoon finely chopped fresh rosemary

Freshly ground black pepper

1 tablespoon plus 2 teaspoons olive oil

2 (1- to 1¼-pound) pork tenderloins

1 tablespoon unsalted butter

For the jam: In a large heavy skillet, heat the butter and oil over medium heat until the butter is melted. Add the onions and ¼ teaspoon salt, reduce the heat to medium-low, and cook, stirring frequently, until the onions are very tender and sweet, 30 to 35 minutes.

Add the maple syrup and bourbon, increase the heat to medium, and cook, stirring occasionally, until the liquid has evaporated and the onions are jammy, about 10 minutes. Remove from the heat. Stir in the pepper and ¼ teaspoon salt, then adjust the seasoning to taste. Serve warm or at room temperature. (*The jam can be made ahead, cooled, covered, and refrigerated for up to 2 weeks.*)

Meanwhile, for the pork: While the jam cooks, mound the garlic with 1 teaspoon salt on a cutting board. Using a chef's knife, mash and chop into a paste. Transfer to a small bowl. Stir in the mustard, rosemary, ½ teaspoon pepper, and 2 teaspoons of the oil.

With a paring knife, make twelve X-shaped incisions, about ⅛ inch deep, all over each tenderloin. Rub the tenderloins all over with the garlic mixture, stuffing bits into the incisions.

Heat the oven to 425°F, with a rack in the middle.

In a large ovenproof skillet, heat the butter and remaining tablespoon oil over medium-high heat until the butter is melted and foamy. Add one tenderloin and cook until browned on the bottom, 5 to 7 minutes. Transfer to a plate and brown the second tenderloin. Return the first tenderloin to the pan and turn them both browned side up.

Transfer the skillet to the oven and roast until an instant-read thermometer inserted into the thickest part of the pork reads 135°F, 15 to 20 minutes. Transfer to a cutting board and let rest for 10 minutes.

Cut the pork into thick slices and serve with the onion jam.

Macadamia-Crusted Lamb Lollies

with Spicy Honey Agrodolce

Serves 4

This recipe was born during a family holiday in Hawaii. My father came home from Costco, his special happy place, with a package of New Zealand rack of spring lamb and a massive bag of macadamia nuts, Hawaii's state nut. Knowing I had a week to use up the contents of the bag (or he would take it back home to Vermont with him and let the nuts sit in his freezer for a decade), I decided to make a crust for the meat with them. Cutting the rack into individual chops speeds up the cooking time and allows for greater coverage of the crushed nut mix. A quick agrodolce, an addictive Italian sauce that's terrific on anything meaty, lends a welcome kick of spice, balanced by a little sweetness and tang.

LAMB

¾ cup macadamia nuts

2 tablespoons finely chopped fresh flat-leaf parsley

1 teaspoon ground coriander

Kosher salt

12 lamb rib chops (about 3 ounces each)

2 teaspoons olive oil

SPICY HONEY AGRODOLCE

½ cup honey

1½ teaspoons finely chopped fresh rosemary

1 teaspoon red pepper flakes

¼ cup red wine vinegar

Kosher salt

For the lamb: Heat the oven to 400°F, with a rack in the middle.

To make the crust, spread the nuts on a rimmed baking sheet and bake until lightly golden, 6 to 8 minutes. Transfer to a plate and let cool completely.

Combine the cooled nuts, parsley, coriander, and ⅛ teaspoon salt in a food processor and pulse until the mixture is finely chopped. Spread the mixture onto a large plate. Set aside.

For the agrodolce: In a small saucepan, heat the honey, rosemary, and red pepper flakes over low heat just until barely warm to the touch, about 3 minutes. Remove from the heat and stir in the vinegar and a pinch of salt. Set aside.

Season the lamb chops on both sides with salt. Heat a large cast-iron skillet or grill pan over medium-high heat until very hot. Brush with the oil. Cook the lamb chops on the fatty edges until browned and crisp, about 2 minutes. Then cook for 2 minutes on each side for medium-rare. Remove the chops from the pan and let rest for 5 minutes, then press both sides of each chop into the nut mixture.

Arrange the chops on a serving platter and drizzle with the agrodolce.

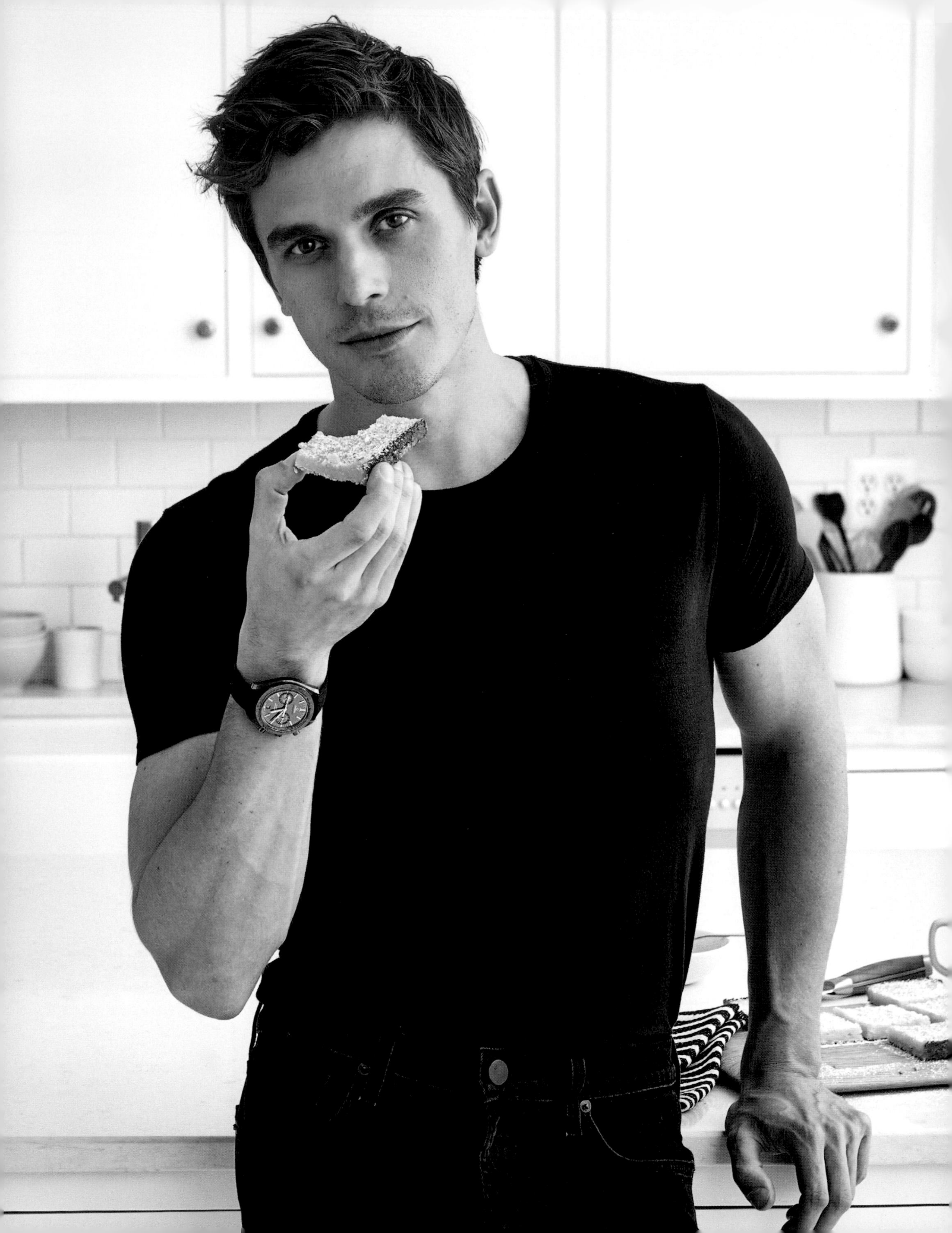

BAKES

Peanut Butter and Nutella Balls

Makes 24 pieces

I'm not gonna dance around this: Most of my late teens and twenties were spent high. During my love affair with the ole devil's lettuce, the munchies demanded as little prepping or cooking as humanly possible. Cue my peanut butter and Nutella balls. Two spoons, a cookie sheet, and a freezer are all the equipment you need for these puppies. I can almost taste my youth whenever I make them. On the romantic side, this treat is also the marriage of two iconic spreads, crunchy peanut butter and Nutella. A topping of crushed pretzels or Skor bars brings it all home with an added layer of flavor and crunch.

---

1 cup (about 12 ounces) Nutella

½ cup crunchy peanut butter, chilled

¼ cup plus 2 tablespoons crushed salty pretzels or Skor bars

A commercial peanut butter like Skippy works best for these confections.

Line a cookie sheet with parchment paper.

Place 2 teaspoons of the Nutella in a regular teaspoon and 1 teaspoon of the peanut butter in another teaspoon.

Gently press the spoon of Nutella against the peanut butter and scoop the peanut butter onto the spoon with the Nutella, then scrape the Nutella–peanut butter mixture back onto the empty spoon. Repeat several times until you have a smooth, football-shaped combo of the two spreads (this is called a quenelle). Ideally the Nutella will cover the peanut butter (this is why you chill the peanut butter—chilling keeps the peanut butter stable while the room-temp Nutella swirls around it), but if it all swirls together, no matter. Drop your little football on the prepared baking sheet and sprinkle about ¾ teaspoon of the crushed pretzels on top. Repeat to make a total of 24 balls.

Freeze the balls until the Nutella is set, about 1 hour. Eat straight from the freezer.

Chewy Chocolate Chunk Cookies

Makes 2 dozen cookies

My loving Auntie Leslie's staple dessert was wonderfully thin chocolate chip cookies chock-full of big old chunks of milk chocolate. They stayed perfectly chewy for days. Her recipe inspired this version, in which a blend of granulated and dark brown sugars lends a subtle caramel-toffee note. Serve the cookies warm or at room temperature with a tall glass of ice-cold milk.

---

2 cups all-purpose flour

1¾ teaspoons kosher salt

¾ teaspoon baking soda

12 tablespoons unsalted butter (1½ sticks), melted and cooled *completely*

½ cup plus 2 tablespoons packed dark brown sugar

½ cup granulated sugar

1 large egg

1 large egg yolk

2 teaspoons pure vanilla extract

11 ounces good-quality milk chocolate, chopped into ¼- to ½-inch pieces (2 cups)

Milk chocolate bars vary in quality and flavor (some are fruity, some are sweeter than others, some are ultra-smooth, and so on). Use one that you love the taste of as an eating chocolate, and it'll work perfectly here too. My favorites include TCHO, Dagoba, and Scharffen Berger.

In a medium bowl, whisk together the flour, salt, and baking soda. In a large bowl, mix together the butter and both sugars by hand until thoroughly blended, then whisk in the egg, egg yolk, and vanilla until well combined. Add the dry ingredients and mix until just combined. Stir in the chocolate chunks. Cover the dough and refrigerate for at least 30 minutes, or as long as overnight. (Chilling deepens the flavor and keeps the cookies from spreading too much when baked.) When ready to bake, if the dough was chilled overnight, let stand at room temperature for 15 minutes, or until it is soft enough to scoop.

Heat the oven to 325°F, with racks in the upper and lower thirds. Line two cookie sheets with parchment paper.

Roll 2-tablespoon portions of dough into balls and place on the baking sheets, spacing the balls 2 inches apart. Flatten with your palm to ½-inch-thick rounds.

Bake, rotating the pans and switching their positions on the racks halfway through, until the cookies are puffed and the tops appear dry, 15 to 17 minutes. Or, if you like crisp cookies, bake until the edges are just golden, 22 to 24 minutes. Let cool slightly on the baking sheets, then transfer the parchment sheets to wire racks and let the cookies cool until just warm or completely cooled.

Salty Lemon Squares (page 238)

Makes sixteen 2-inch squares

I spent a couple of summers when I was young in Knowlton, Quebec, where my Auntie Magda had a summer home she ran as an unofficial sleepaway camp for all of the cousins. Our carefree days were spent horseback riding, face painting, running about in the yard, and, of course, eating. Auntie Madga was a fantastic cook who put a touch of Polish in every dish. Her daughter, Maïa, two years my elder, likely inspired by her mum, was a passionate young baker. Maïa spent most of her mornings in the kitchen, baking something delicious so that we could all have treats after lunch. That first summer at "cousins' camp," she was obsessed with lemon squares. Brand-new to me, they were sweet and tangy, bright and cookie-like, and I ate them with abandon. But what also struck me was the idea that cooking is not necessarily a chore that somebody else does for you while you're playing outside. If you love cooking, it's fun. Today, whenever I make these lemon bars, which are a slight riff on Maïa's original, I think back to that time that helped shape both my palate and my life path. *The photo is on pages 236–237.*

CRUST

1 cup all-purpose flour

1/4 cup granulated sugar

1/2 teaspoon kosher salt

8 tablespoons (1 stick) unsalted butter, melted and slightly cooled

FILLING

2 large eggs

1 cup granulated sugar

1/2 teaspoon baking powder

Finely grated zest of 1 large or 2 medium lemons (1 1/2 to 2 tablespoons)

1/4 cup fresh lemon juice (from 1 large or 2 medium lemons)

Confectioners' sugar for dusting

Flaky sea salt, such as Maldon, for sprinkling

Heat the oven to 350°F, with a rack in the middle. Line an 8-inch square baking pan with two sheets of foil, shiny side up, crisscrossing them to leave an overhang on all sides. Lightly spray with nonstick cooking spray or grease with butter.

For the crust: In a large bowl, whisk together the flour, sugar, and salt. Add the cooled melted butter and stir to combine. Turn the mixture out into the baking pan and press evenly over the bottom. Bake until the edges are just beginning to brown, 18 to 22 minutes.

Meanwhile, make the filling: With an electric mixer, beat the eggs in a medium bowl until combined. Add the granulated sugar, baking powder, lemon zest, and lemon juice and beat on medium-high until the mixture is frothy, 2 to 3 minutes.

Pour the filling into the hot crust. Return the pan to the oven and bake until the filling is just set, 22 to 25 minutes. Let cool completely in the pan on a wire rack, at least 1½ hours. For the best flavor and easiest cutting, chill in the refrigerator at least 4 hours, or up to 1 day. (*The bars can be covered and refrigerated for up to 3 days or frozen for up to 1 month. Thaw, unwrapped, for 1 hour at room temperature before serving.*)

To serve, cut the bars into 2-inch squares, then dust with confectioners' sugar and sprinkle with flaky salt.

Tips

After grating the lemons, warm them in the microwave for 5- to 10-second intervals until just a bit warm, 15 to 30 seconds, which will help release the most juice.

The flavor of these bars deepens overnight, so make them a day ahead if you can.

Makes about 4 dozen cookies

Ginger-Cardamom Cowboy Cookies

I love my castmate Tan for many reasons, but at the top of the list is his indulgent nature and the fact that he never denies himself a good cookie or slice of cake, no matter the time of day. This variation on his chocolate-ginger favorites includes warm notes of cardamom as a nod to his Brit-Pakistani heritage. And Tan's husband is a legit cowboy.

---

1 cup pecans

2 cups old-fashioned oats

1¼ cups all-purpose flour

1 teaspoon baking soda

¾ teaspoon kosher salt

½ teaspoon ground cardamom

12 tablespoons (1½ sticks) unsalted butter, softened

1 cup plus 3 tablespoons packed light brown sugar

2 large eggs

1 teaspoon pure vanilla extract

1 cup bittersweet chocolate chips

¾ cup coarsely chopped candied ginger

½ cup shredded unsweetened coconut

Heat the oven to 350°F, with a rack in the middle.

Spread the pecans on a baking sheet and bake until fragrant and toasted, about 8 minutes. Transfer the pecans to a plate and let cool completely, then coarsely chop.

In a medium bowl, whisk together the oats, flour, baking soda, salt, and cardamom. With an electric mixer, beat together the butter and sugar in a large bowl at medium speed until light and fluffy, 2 to 3 minutes. Add the eggs and vanilla and beat until blended, scraping down the sides of the bowl once or twice. Add the oat mixture and beat at low speed to combine. Fold in the chocolate chips, candied ginger, coconut, and pecans.

Cover and refrigerate the dough for at least 30 minutes, or as long as overnight. (Chilling deepens the flavor and keeps the cookies from spreading too much when baked.) If you chilled the dough overnight, let it stand at room temperature for 45 minutes or so, until it is soft enough to scoop.

When ready to bake, heat the oven to 350°F, with racks in the middle and lower thirds. Line two cookie sheets with parchment paper.

Drop the dough by heaping tablespoons onto the baking sheets, spacing them 1½ inches apart. Bake, rotating the pans and switching their positions on the racks halfway through, until the edges are golden, about 16 minutes. Let the cookies cool on the pans on wire racks for 5 minutes, then transfer to the racks to cool completely. Reuse the parchment for the next batches.

Polish Caramel Easter Squares
(page 244)

Polish Caramel Easter Squares

Makes 16 squares

These bar cookies are most often served at Easter time in Polish homes, though I've seen them at Christmas and New Year's. There are a number of variations, from lemon, orange, and chocolate to crushed nuts, but this classic caramel is by far my favorite. I make it with a hazelnut crust, which lends a delicious nutty-toasty flavor. Decorating the top in the traditional way with hazelnuts, dried apricots, golden raisins, and sliced almonds is pretty and a great sign of respect to the Polish motherland. *The photo is on pages 242–243.*

CRUST

½ cup unblanched hazelnuts, plus 16 skin-on nuts for garnish

1½ cups all-purpose flour

¼ cup plus 2 tablespoons sugar

½ teaspoon kosher salt

12 tablespoons (1½ sticks) unsalted butter, melted and cooled

APRICOT JAM LAYER

¼ cup apricot preserves

CARAMEL

2 cups sugar

1 cup plus 3 tablespoons heavy cream, at room temperature

1 tablespoon unsalted butter

½ teaspoon pure vanilla extract

½ teaspoon kosher salt

TOPPING

2 tablespoons sliced almonds

7 dried apricots, cut into thin strips

¼ cup golden raisins

For the crust: Heat the oven to 350°F, with a rack in the middle. Line an 8-inch square baking pan with two sheets of foil, shiny side up, crisscrossing them to leave an overhang on all sides. Lightly spray with nonstick cooking spray or grease with butter.

Spread the nuts on a baking sheet and bake until fragrant and toasted, 10 to 12 minutes. Remove the nuts from the oven and let cool for 10 minutes. Set aside 16 nuts for garnish and wrap the remaining nuts in a clean kitchen towel. Reduce the oven temperature to 325°F.

Rub the warm nuts in the towel to remove most of the skins (it's OK if they don't all come off). Transfer to a food processor and pulse until very finely chopped, then transfer to a medium bowl.

Add the flour, sugar, and salt to the chopped nuts and whisk to combine. Add the cooled melted butter and stir to combine. Turn the mixture out into the prepared baking pan and press it evenly over the bottom and ¼ inch up the sides. Bake until lightly golden, 30 to 35 minutes. Let cool completely on a wire rack. (The crust will firm up as it cools.)

For the apricot jam layer: Heat the preserves in a small saucepan over low heat just until warm to the touch and loose enough to spread easily, 1 to 2 minutes. Brush the warm jam over the cooled crust. Set aside.

For the caramel: Place the sugar in a large deep saucepan. Slowly and evenly pour ¼ cup plus 2 tablespoons water over the sugar to moisten it evenly. Heat over medium-low heat, undisturbed, until the sugar is a deep amber-brown, 12 to 15 minutes. Brush down the sides of the pan with a wet pastry brush if necessary to remove any sugar crystals.

In a medium saucepan, heat the cream, butter, vanilla, and salt until the cream is warm and the butter is melted. Remove from the heat.

Toward the end of cooking the caramel, gently swirl the pan to ensure that the sugar caramelizes evenly. If at any point the sugar bubbles so much that you can't see the color, reduce the heat to low.

Remove the pan from the heat. Carefully add the cream mixture (the mixture will bubble up), stirring with a whisk or silicone spatula to combine. Fit the pot with a candy thermometer and return it to medium heat. Cook the caramel, whisking occasionally, until it reaches 245°F, 4 to 6 minutes. Remove from the heat and immediately pour it over the hazelnut crust, tilting the pan as needed to spread it evenly. Let cool on a wire rack for 1 hour, then refrigerate until the caramel is set, at least 1 hour, or overnight.

For the topping: Using the foil, remove the bar from the pan. Peel off the foil, then cut the bar into 16 squares. Decorate the bars with the sliced almonds, apricots, reserved hazelnuts, and raisins to make flowers, or as you like. The bars keep, covered and refrigerated, for up to 1 week. Serve at room temperature.

Strawberry–Pink Peppercorn Eton Mess

Serves 6

This dessert is really about simplicity. A bowl of perfect summer fruit, made even more perfect with an imperfect mess of whipped cream and chunks of meringue. An uncomplicated, delicious, and beautiful mess.

MERINGUE

2 large egg whites, at room temperature

1/4 cup granulated sugar

1/4 cup confectioners' sugar

1/4 teaspoon pure vanilla extract

1/4 teaspoon kosher salt

1/4 teaspoon pink peppercorns, crushed

BERRIES AND CREAM

2 pounds strawberries, hulled and cut into bite-sized pieces (set aside 6 whole berries for the garnish)

3/4 teaspoon granulated sugar

1 1/2 teaspoons orange-flavored liqueur, such as Cointreau or Grand Marnier (optional; see Tip)

1 3/4 cups heavy cream

1 tablespoon confectioners' sugar

Crushed pink peppercorns for garnish

For the meringue: Heat the oven to 275°F, with a rack in the middle. Line a baking sheet with parchment paper.

With an electric mixer, beat the egg whites in a medium bowl on medium-high speed until foamy, about 1 minute. With the mixer running, slowly add the granulated sugar and then continue beating until the mixture is shiny, has tripled in volume, and holds stiff peaks, 8 to 10 minutes. Add the confectioners' sugar, vanilla, and salt and beat just to blend.

Using a rubber spatula, fold in the pink peppercorns. Spread the meringue evenly onto the baking sheet to about 1/4 inch thick. Bake until the meringue is lightly golden, 50 to 60 minutes. Test by ripping off a small piece and letting it stand at room temperature for 10 seconds. If it is dry and crunchy throughout, it is done. It may still feel a little tacky, but it will dry as it cools. Remove the meringue from the oven and cool completely on the baking sheet on a wire rack, about 30 minutes.

Break the cooled meringue into small pieces. (*The meringue can be made up to 5 days ahead and stored airtight at cool dry room temperature.*)

Tip The orange liqueur adds another level of flavor to the berries, but you can use leftover bubbles (Champagne, cava, or Prosecco), or a splash of any other liqueur you like, or skip it altogether.

For the berries and cream: In a medium bowl, toss together the strawberries with the granulated sugar and liqueur, if using. With an electric mixer, beat the heavy cream and confectioners' sugar in a large bowl to medium peaks.

Divide about half of the berry mixture among six serving glasses or bowls. Top each with a few pieces of meringue. Spoon about half of the whipped cream on top. Repeat with a second layer of meringue, berries, and cream. Top each serving with a whole berry and a pinch of crushed pink peppercorns. Serve immediately.

Vanilla Pots de Crème

with Mango Coulis

Serves 6

There's something so damn adorable about a single-serve dessert in a cute little pot with its own lid, the traditional presentation for pots de crème (ramekins work just as well). This has been my dessert choice at every French restaurant since I can remember. The creamy but dense vanilla base gets a lift from the bright floral tang of a fresh mango coulis, a small spin on a true classic.

POTS DE CRÈME

1½ cups heavy cream

¼ cup plus 2 tablespoons whole milk

½ teaspoon pure vanilla extract

⅛ teaspoon kosher salt

5 large egg yolks

3 tablespoons sugar

MANGO COULIS

1 cup coarsely chopped ripe mango (about ½ large mango)

1 tablespoon fresh lime juice

½ teaspoon sugar

FOR SERVING

⅓ cup heavy cream

For the pots de crème: Heat the oven to 300°F, with a rack in the middle.

In a medium saucepan, heat the cream, milk, vanilla extract, and salt over medium heat, stirring occasionally, until the mixture just comes to a simmer. Meanwhile, in a medium bowl, vigorously whisk the egg yolks and sugar until the mixture is thick and pale yellow, about 4 minutes.

Remove the cream mixture from the heat and, whisking constantly, very slowly add it to the egg yolk mixture. Transfer the mixture to a 4-cup liquid measure or pitcher. Divide among six 4-ounce ramekins.

Set the ramekins in a 9-x-13-inch Pyrex baking dish or baking pan. Add just enough boiling water to come halfway up the sides of the ramekins. Bake the custards until they are just set (they should still be a bit wobbly in the center when shaken), 30 to 35 minutes.

Remove the pan from the oven and let the pots de crème cool in the water bath for 5 minutes, then transfer the ramekins to a wire rack and let cool completely, about 1 hour. Refrigerate until cold, at least 4 hours, or overnight; the crème will firm as it cools. (*The pots de crème can be made up to 5 days ahead and kept covered in the refrigerator.*)

Meanwhile, for the mango coulis: In a blender or food processor, combine the mango, lime juice, and sugar and puree until smooth. Transfer to a bowl, cover, and chill until ready to serve. (*The coulis can be made up to 8 hours ahead.*)

For serving: Let the pots de crème stand at room temperature for about 30 minutes to take the chill off. In a small bowl, beat the cream to soft peaks. Top the pots with the cold coulis. Spoon a little whipped cream on top and serve.

Challah White Chocolate–Raspberry Bread Pudding

Serves 6 to 8

I. Love. Bread pudding. I love how simple it is to make a nice custard, which then gets soaked up by cubes of sweet, golden challah. I love that it's a little Jewish (well, my version is). I love how the pudding rises a little when it bakes and gets even more golden. I love the contrast of crispy crust and creamy filling, and I especially love this combo of melty white chocolate and fresh raspberries.

---

1 tablespoon unsalted butter, softened

2 tablespoons turbinado or demerara sugar

6 cups 1½-inch cubes day-old challah (about 14 ounces)

2 cups (9½ ounces) fresh raspberries

3 large eggs

1 large egg yolk

½ teaspoon kosher salt

2 cups whole milk

½ cup granulated sugar

1 teaspoon pure vanilla extract

4 ounces white chocolate, chopped into ¼- to ½-inch chunks

Heat the oven to 375°F, with a rack in the middle. Butter an 8-inch square baking pan (or a 1½- to 2-quart gratin dish) with the softened butter, then sprinkle with 1 tablespoon of the turbinado or demerara sugar.

Place the bread cubes and raspberries in a large bowl. In a medium heatproof bowl, whisk together the eggs, egg yolk, and salt.

Combine the milk, granulated sugar, and vanilla in a large saucepan and heat over medium heat, whisking to dissolve the sugar, just until the mixture comes to a bare simmer. Remove from the heat.

Whisking constantly, gradually pour about one third of the milk mixture into the egg mixture. Again whisking constantly, pour the egg mixture back into the milk mixture to combine. Pour the mixture over the bread and berries and stir to coat the bread cubes.

Scrape the bread mixture into the baking dish. Sprinkle with the chopped white chocolate, pushing about half of the chocolate pieces about ½ inch into the crevices in the bread mixture. Sprinkle with the remaining tablespoon of turbinado or demerara sugar.

Tip Challah is a traditional Jewish yeast bread enriched with eggs. Its sweet, buttery flavor and light, airy texture are similar to brioche, which you can easily substitute. Other good breads for bread pudding include Pullman sandwich loaf and French bread. The latter is chewier than the other three, so your dessert will have a denser texture.

Cover the pan with foil, sealing the edges, and bake for 25 minutes. Carefully uncover the dish, rotate it, and continue baking until the custard is set and the top is golden and crisp, 20 to 30 minutes more.

Serve the pudding hot, right from the oven. The pudding is best on the day it is baked, but it can be made ahead, cooled, and kept covered and refrigerated for up to 3 days; rewarm in a 350°F oven for 10 minutes.

Raspberry Mousse Dome

Serves 12

My mum's skills in the kitchen skew toward savory. An amazing home cook, she admits to being a bit lacking in the dessert department. That said, she does have a "treat trick" or two up her sleeve. Her easy-to-make, no-fail reliable—and our family favorite—is this dessert. I remember the excitement around the unmolding of the dome and the way my sisters and I would look on in anticipation. Then she'd let us help create pretty patterns with fruits and chocolate that weren't unlike the folk designs on Polish polka dresses, table linens, and pottery. Now the dome, as I call it, is *my* favored finale. With its bright pink interior, crackly chocolate shell, tangy berries, and fresh mint leaves, it's a guaranteed showstopper.

DOME

6 cups frozen raspberries (24 ounces)

1/2 cup sugar

2 tablespoons unflavored powdered gelatin (from three 1/4-ounce envelopes)

3 cups heavy cream

CHOCOLATE SHELL

4 ounces bittersweet chocolate, coarsely chopped (3/4 cup)

1/4 cup coconut oil, melted

1/4 teaspoon kosher salt

FOR SERVING

6 ounces fresh raspberries (about 1 3/4 cups)

6 ounces fresh blackberries (about 1 1/2 cups)

Fresh mint leaves

For the dome: Line a 10-cup (2½-quart) metal bowl with plastic wrap, crisscrossing two pieces if necessary, leaving an overhang all around.

Put the raspberries in a large saucepan and warm over low heat, stirring occasionally, until thawed and a little juicy, about 5 minutes. Transfer to a fine-mesh sieve set over a large bowl and press on the berries to extract all the juice. You should have 1½ cups juice. Discard the seeds. Add the sugar to the juice and whisk to combine.

Continues

Pour ¼ cup tepid water into a small saucepan and sprinkle the gelatin over the top. Let stand for 5 minutes.

Heat the gelatin mixture over medium-low heat, stirring frequently, just until dissolved, about 2 minutes. Remove the gelatin from the heat and stir into the raspberry mixture. Let stand, stirring occasionally, until the mixture has thickened to the consistency of raw egg whites, about 20 to 25 minutes. (If the mixture becomes too thick, gently warm it over a pot of boiling water, then cool, stirring, to the proper consistency.)

With an electric mixer, beat the cream in a large bowl to medium peaks (just barely stiff). Fold about one quarter of the whipped cream into the raspberry mixture to lighten it, then fold in the remaining whipped cream. Pour the mixture into the prepared bowl. Refrigerate, covered, until set, at least 8 hours, or overnight.

When ready to serve, make the chocolate shell: Combine the chocolate, coconut oil, and salt in a medium microwave-safe bowl. Microwave for 15-second intervals, stirring well between each, until the mixture is smooth, 1 to 1½ minutes. Let cool to room temperature, about 15 minutes.

Invert the dome onto a platter, then remove the bowl and plastic wrap. Slowly pour about ½ cup of the cooled chocolate shell over the cold dome, guiding and gently smoothing it over the dome with the back of a spoon as you go. Let stand until the chocolate has hardened, 5 to 10 minutes. (If the coating cracks, use the remaining chocolate to fill in and repair it.)

For serving: Decorate the dome as you wish with some of the fruit and mint.

Run a large chef's knife under hot tap water, then wipe dry. Use the hot knife, wiping it clean between cuts and rewarming it if necessary, to cut the dome into wedges. Serve with the remaining fruit and mint.

Watermelon Ginger Tower

Serves 6

I'm not sure how this idea came about, but ever since the day I had watermelon kissed with ginger and mint, I haven't been able to go back to plain-Jane melon. The kid in me loves to cut it into same-size cubes and stack them in a Jenga tower on pretty plates. The dessert is refreshing when you want something light to end a meal. However you'd like to cut, cube, stack, ball, or otherwise serve the melon is absolutely A-OK. Just promise me you'll try it.

12 cups 1-inch cubes seedless watermelon (from a 10-pound watermelon)

1 teaspoon finely grated peeled fresh ginger

¼ cup fresh mint leaves, ideally tiny ones, torn or sliced if larger

In a large bowl, gently toss together the watermelon cubes and ginger. On a large platter or on individual serving plates, stack the cubes Jenga-style, then sprinkle with the mint. Or arrange the melon in whatever way makes you very happy and then sprinkle. Serve.

Tip Purchasing very fresh ginger and using a Microplane rasp grater to grate it are the keys here. The very fine grate brings out the pungent ginger juices and allows the shreds to best meld with the watermelon.

Jim's Pi Pie

Serves 8

During the seven wonderful, heart-opening years I spent with my former boyfriend, Joey, we marked each birthday with a celebratory sweet. One year, shortly before my twenty-something, Joey's father, Jim—who is such a great baker we joked that he would be perfect as a competitor on *The Great British Baking Show*—asked me to name my dream birthday dessert. (One of my favorite sorts of questions, BTW.) I quickly made it up on the spot: a salty graham cracker crust covered with a layer of caramely dulce de leche, then topped with creamy chocolate custard and a puff of golden, swirly baked meringue. A few weeks later, on my birthday, Jim and Minette, Joey's mom, arrived with a fresh-baked rendition of that very dessert. Since my birthday is March 14—National Pi Day—we named it Jim's Pi Pie. I ate half of it that night. It truly is the dreamiest pie ever.

CRUST

11 plain graham crackers, broken into small pieces (about 4 cups)

2 tablespoons packed dark brown sugar

1 tablespoon all-purpose flour

½ teaspoon kosher salt

7 tablespoons unsalted butter, melted

FILLING

5 ounces bittersweet chocolate, finely chopped (about 1 cup)

4 ounces unsweetened chocolate, finely chopped (scant 1 cup)

1 cup granulated sugar

6 large egg yolks

½ cup cornstarch

¾ teaspoon kosher salt

4½ cups whole milk

3 tablespoons unsalted butter, cut into small pieces, softened

1 teaspoon pure vanilla extract

1 (13.4-ounce) can dulce de leche

MERINGUE

4 large egg whites, at room temperature

⅛ teaspoon cream of tartar

¼ cup plus 2 tablespoons granulated sugar

Continues

For the crust: Heat the oven to 350°F, with a rack in the middle.

Place the graham crackers in a food processor. Add the brown sugar, flour, and salt and pulse until fine crumbs form. With the machine running, add the melted butter and process just until combined. Transfer the mixture to a deep-dish 9-inch pie plate and press evenly over the bottom and up the sides. Freeze for 10 minutes.

Place the pie plate on a baking sheet and bake, rotating the pan once halfway through, until the crust is set, 10 to 12 minutes. Let cool on a wire rack, about 15 minutes.

For the filling: In a heatproof bowl set over a saucepan of barely simmering water (the bowl should not touch the water), melt the chocolates, stirring until smooth. Remove the bowl from the heat.

In a medium saucepan, whisk together the sugar, egg yolks, cornstarch, and salt to combine well. Whisking constantly, slowly add the milk. Whisking constantly, bring the mixture just to a boil over medium heat. Reduce to a simmer and cook, whisking constantly, until the custard is thick, 1 to 2 minutes.

Set a fine-mesh sieve over a bowl and strain the custard into the bowl. Whisk in the melted chocolate, butter, and vanilla until smooth. Cover the surface of the custard with plastic wrap (to prevent a skin from forming) and let cool completely, about 1 hour.

Pour the dulce de leche into the crust, spreading it to cover the bottom. Pour the chocolate filling into the crust. Chill the pie, covered, for at least 6 hours, or overnight.

For the meringue: Heat the oven to 500°F, with a rack in the middle.

With an electric mixer, beat the egg whites and cream of tartar in a large bowl on medium speed until frothy, about 3 minutes. With the mixer on medium-high, slowly add the sugar, then continue beating to stiff, glossy peaks, 2 to 3 minutes more.

Decoratively swirl the meringue on top of the pie, being sure to spread it to the edges of the crust to completely cover the filling. To toast the meringue, place the pie on the oven rack and bake, watching closely to avoid burning, until the meringue is golden in spots, about 3 minutes. Alternatively, you can use a kitchen butane torch.

Cut the pie into wedges and serve. The pie is best the day it is baked, but for longer keeping, insert a few toothpicks into the meringue an inch or two from the edges of the pie and loosely cover with plastic wrap. Refrigerate for up to 2 days.

Serves 12 to 15

Kansas City Coconut Sheet Cake

Beth Barden, a successful restaurateur in Kansas City, Missouri, who became a caterer for *Queer Eye* there, loves to play with American classics like sheet cake. This is one of her best. It's such a perfect cake for a crowd, and it always makes me think of children's birthday parties. Whipped ricotta lightens the sugar load on the frosting for this coconut version, which is topped with lots of flaky coconut. *The photo is on page 261.*

CAKE

1/2 cup unrefined coconut oil, melted and cooled, plus more for greasing the pan

2 1/2 cups all-purpose flour

2 teaspoons baking powder

1/2 teaspoon kosher salt

1 cup full-fat coconut milk, well shaken before measuring

1/2 cup plain nonfat Greek yogurt

Finely grated zest of 1 large lemon (about 1 1/2 tablespoons)

1 tablespoon fresh lemon juice

1 teaspoon pure vanilla extract

1 1/2 cups granulated sugar

8 tablespoons (1 stick) unsalted butter, softened

4 large eggs, at room temperature

1 cup sweetened shredded coconut

COCONUT WHIPPED CREAM FROSTING

2 cups packaged unsweetened flaked coconut

1 (15-ounce) container part-skim ricotta (about 1 3/4 cups)

1/2 cup confectioners' sugar

2 cups heavy cream

1/2 teaspoon pure vanilla extract

Tip

Be sure to use unrefined coconut oil here. If the oil is refined, it loses its nutty taste.

For the cake: Heat the oven to 350°F, with a rack in the middle. Grease a 9-x-13-inch baking pan with coconut oil.

In a medium bowl, whisk together the flour, baking powder, and salt. In a second medium bowl, whisk together the coconut milk, yogurt, lemon zest and juice, and vanilla.

Continues

With an electric mixer, beat the coconut oil, sugar, and butter in a large bowl on medium speed, scraping down the sides occasionally, until smooth, about 3 minutes. Add the eggs one at a time, beating well after each addition. Add the coconut milk mixture and beat until well combined, about 2 minutes (the mixture may appear curdled). Reduce the speed to low and add the flour mixture in two additions, mixing just to combine. Fold in the coconut with a rubber spatula, making sure to fully incorporate it.

Scrape the batter into the prepared pan and spread it evenly with the spatula. Bake until the cake is lightly golden on top and a cake tester inserted in the center comes out clean, 35 to 40 minutes, rotating the pan halfway through. Remove the cake from the oven and cool completely in the pan on a wire rack. (Leave the oven on.)

Meanwhile, make the frosting: Spread the coconut in a single layer on a baking sheet and bake until golden and fragrant, 5 to 7 minutes. Let cool completely in the pan on a wire rack.

With an electric mixer, beat together the ricotta and confectioners' sugar in a large bowl on medium-high until the sugar is dissolved and the cheese is creamy, 3 to 5 minutes. Add the cream and vanilla and beat until soft peaks form, about 3 minutes. Gently fold in 1 cup of the toasted coconut. Cover the frosting and chill until it sets a bit, at least 30 minutes, and up to 4 hours. Set the remaining coconut aside.

Spread the frosting over the top of the cake. Sprinkle with the reserved toasted coconut. Cut the cake into pieces and serve. The cake can be kept, covered and refrigerated, for up to 3 days.

Olive Oil–Pecan Streusel Bundt Cake

with Brown Butter Glaze

Serves 8 to 10

This coffee cake marries a classic streusel with the light crumb of an olive oil cake, adding a brown butter glaze that slinks down the sides. It's a great breakfast, brunch, or afternoon indulgence.

STREUSEL

1½ cups pecans (6 ounces), finely chopped

½ cup packed dark brown sugar

1 tablespoon ground cinnamon

½ teaspoon kosher salt

3 tablespoons unsalted butter, melted and cooled

CAKE

2 cups all-purpose flour

2 teaspoons baking powder

1 teaspoon kosher salt

1¼ cups granulated sugar

3 large eggs, at room temperature

1 tablespoon finely grated lemon zest (from 1 large lemon)

1 cup extra-virgin olive oil

⅔ cup sour cream

GLAZE

3 tablespoons unsalted butter

¾ cup plus 2 tablespoons confectioners' sugar

1 teaspoon pure vanilla extract

2 to 3 tablespoons whole milk

For the streusel: Heat the oven to 350°F, with a rack in the middle.

Spread the pecans on a baking sheet and bake until fragrant and toasted, about 5 minutes. Transfer to a plate and let cool completely. (Leave the oven on.)

In a large bowl, mix the pecans with the brown sugar, cinnamon, and salt, breaking up any clumps of brown sugar with your fingers. Stir in the butter to combine.

For the cake: Butter and flour a 10-cup nonstick Bundt pan.

In a medium bowl, whisk together the flour, baking powder, and salt. In a large bowl, whisk together the sugar, eggs, and lemon zest until the sugar is mostly dissolved and the mixture is pale and frothy, about 2 minutes. Whisk in the oil and sour cream. Using a rubber spatula, stir in the flour mixture until the batter is smooth and no dry flour streaks remain.

Continues

Pour one third of the batter into the prepared pan. Sprinkle with half of the streusel. Gently tap the pan on the counter to settle the batter. Repeat with half of the remaining batter and all the remaining streusel, then top with the remaining batter. Smooth the top, then gently tap the pan on the counter to settle the batter one last time. Bake, rotating the pan halfway through, until the edges of the cake pull away from the sides and the cake springs back from a light touch, 45 to 50 minutes.

Let the cake cool in the pan on a wire rack for 15 minutes, then gently invert it onto a wire rack and lift off the pan. Let cool completely, about 2 hours.

For the glaze: Heat the butter in a small saucepan over medium heat, stirring, until melted and just golden brown, 4 to 6 minutes. Immediately transfer the butter to a heatproof bowl, leaving most of the browned bits in the pan. Add the confectioners' sugar, vanilla, and 2 tablespoons milk and stir until smooth. Add more milk if needed to thin the glaze to a pourable consistency.

Drizzle the glaze over the cake. Let the glaze set, about 15 minutes, before serving. To serve, cut the cake into wedges.

This cake tastes even better after sitting for a day, unglazed and covered, at room temperature. Glaze it on the day of serving.

NATURE COSMETIC
AT&T

Index

Note: Page references in *italics* indicate photographs.

P